Self-Esteem

COPING THROUGH

Self-

Esteem

Rhoda McFarland

THE ROSEN PUBLISHING GROUP, INC./ NEW YORK

Published in *1988* by The Rosen Publishing Group, Inc.
29 East 21st Street, New York, NY 10010

Copyright 1988 by Rhoda McFarland

First Edition

Library of Congress Cataloging-in-Publication Data

McFarland, Rhoda.
     Coping through self-esteem.

     Bibliography: p.
     Includes index.
     Summary: Offers advice on how to build self-esteem in order to deal with everyday problems and relationships in a positive and healthy manner.
     1. Self-respect in teenagers — Juvenile literature.
2. Assertiveness in teenagers — Juvenile literature. [1. Self-respect. 2. Assertiveness (Psychology)] I. Title.
BF724.3.S36M37 1988   158'.1   87-37693
ISBN 0-8239-0790-2

Manufactured in U.S.A

Contents

CHAPTER 1

What Is Self-esteem?

Heart pounding, stomach churning, feeling so scared she thought she would die before she reached her seat, Polly Perfect walked as confidently as she could into her English class. She was late and ·knew all eyes would be on her. She wished she had stopped to brush her hair and to check that her shirt looked all right. She just knew something was wrong with her, and everybody would see it. She put her pass on Mr. Jargon's desk and smiled at Harry Hardy on her way to her seat. She wished Harry would pay more attention to her. It would be wonderful if Harry would like her the way she liked him, but he was so good-looking and self-confident that Polly knew he couldn't possibly be interested in her.

Polly hung around the same crowd that Harry did, but he never made it a point to talk to her. She guessed it was because she wasn't good-looking enough and didn't have a great personality. She didn't go out very much because she had to study to keep her grades up. If she had anything less than an A on her report card, her parents made a big deal out of it. Polly was involved in school activities and was on the track team in the spring, but she wasn't very sure of herself. Even though she was part of a group, she didn't feel really accepted. She felt that the other girls were cuter and had nicer clothes and were so much more confident. They talked to the boys so easily, and even though they complained about some of the teachers, the teachers thought they were wonderful.

All in all, Polly didn't feel very good about herself, and no matter how hard she tried, she never could do anything that made her feel good for very long. She worked so hard to get her parents' approval, but they only noticed what she did wrong. When she dressed for school she spent hours getting every hair in place and making sure that her clothes were just right. She tried to be a good friend so everyone in the group would like her. She even tried to be nice to people who weren't in her crowd because she didn't want anybody to think she was a snob. When teachers asked her to help, she always did. Polly tried very hard to be as perfect as she could be, but she never could be perfect enough.

Even though she apologized when she made a mistake, Polly was sure that people thought she was terrible. She would think for days of the things she could or should have done or said or shouldn't have done or said. Polly remembered every embarrassing thing that ever happened to her, and they all came to mind when she made the tiniest mistake. It was so depressing.

Teachers would tell her what a good job she had done, but Polly knew that she could have done better. Whenever someone told her that what she was wearing was cute, she knew that lots of girls looked better than she did. When her mother's friends commented enviously on her slimness, Polly thought they were just being kind because she knew she was too skinny. It all came down to the fact that Polly felt there was something wrong with her. She could never live up to her own standards and always felt painfully inadequate. Her constant thought was, "What's wrong with me?"

As Polly walked into English class, Harry Hardy thought again how cute she was. She really had everything going for her. She was smart and all the teachers liked her. Everybody in their crowd liked her because she was so friendly and helpful. Harry liked the way she dressed; she looked so put together all the time, not like a ragbag the way some of the girls looked. He thought about asking her out but was sure she would turn him down.

It was easy for Harry to talk to the guys, but he had trouble when it came to girls. He tried to put on a big front as a woman killer, but inside he knew that he wasn't much. The only girls he got involved with were the ones who fell all over him, and anybody who played a decent game of football could have had them. Nice girls like Polly wouldn't give him the time of day, or so he thought.

Ever since Harry could remember, people were on his case about his grades. They kept telling him how bright he was and how much potential he had and how he *should* be getting As. He studied just enough to get Bs so his parents wouldn't get too pushed out of shape, but he knew he wasn't living up to their expectations. What difference did it make? He would never be good enough to suit anybody anyway. Harry made a big show of not caring what anybody thought, but every time a teacher said something about his potential he wanted to put his fist through the wall. He was tired of hearing what a disappointment he was.

Sometimes Harry just wanted to give it all up. He couldn't seem to please anyone. He would play a great game of football, or so he thought, and then his dad would tell him how he missed a block. He knew he didn't get them all, but he didn't like to hear about every one he missed. He told himself about those and didn't need any help. What made it even worse was his mother saying to his father, "Now, leave him alone. Harry's the best lineman on the team. They wouldn't win a single game without him." Harry couldn't decide which was worse, the criticism or the phony praise. The only way he could live with any of it was to pretend that everything was wonderful and nothing bothered him. Around the guys his motto was, "Keep 'em laughin'." He just wished he could do that around girls he liked, girls like Polly.

If only he could feel as good about himself as he pretended he did. Harry put on the happy-go-lucky front so others wouldn't know how bad he felt inside and to fool himself, too. It didn't work. He knew he was a screw-up.

Looking after Polly as she walked to her seat, Harry noticed Brad Brasher giving her a big smile. Brad was always flashing his million-dollar smile. He really thought he was something. If you wanted to know how wonderful he was, you just had to get within ten feet of Brad and he'd tell you. According to Brad, he was able to do or had done everything that could be done. He claimed to ace advanced algebra tests without studying, get the family car whenever he wanted it, have girls calling him every night. Harry figured Brad would claim to leap tall buildings in a single bound.

What Harry didn't know was how Brad felt inside. Brad was all show and no go. Girls didn't call him *any* night, and he had studied very hard and barely pulled a B in the algebra test. Brad felt there was something wrong with him, and he had to cover it up with a lot of noise about how good he was. He didn't like himself, so he pretended to be someone he thought he *could* like or that others *would* like. Brad figured that if others liked him he would be okay.

Polly, Harry, and Brad all had the same problem and showed it differently. They were unsure of themselves and did not like themselves very well. Underlying all their behavior was the same question, "What's wrong with me?" Because they judged themselves so harshly, they thought everyone else did too. When they were very young they had come to believe one of the biggest lies that our society instills: that you must be perfect or you are no good. You see perfect people doing perfect things on TV every day. Commercials tell you that if you aren't perfect you can't be happy, your dog won't like you, your hair won't shine, your teeth will be dull, your neighbors will know you don't wash your dishes with Dishglo, and your friends will be peering over your shoulder to check out the ring around your collar. When you get worried about all that, someone is bound to ask, "What's wrong with you?"

Little children are always being directed, corrected, and expected. So often when you didn't do what you were expected to do you heard, "Why can't you ever do anything right?" You were wrong again, and being wrong is bad; therefore, you felt you must be bad. When you were making mudpies in the yard because the gooshy mud was fun to play with and your mother got excited and demanded, "Why are you making such a mess of yourself?" you didn't know how to answer. Whatever you said would only get you into more trouble for being bad, and you began to think you *were* bad, that there was something wrong with you.

Maybe you were like Polly. She would get all ready for school, and before she could get out the door her mother would stop her and straighten her collar or smooth her hair or tell her to tie her shoelace tighter. She was never quite perfect enough to pass inspection.

Brad Brasher's father would scowl at him and ask if that

was the best he could do. Brad didn't know how to answer. It *was* the best he could do, but he could see by his father's face that it wasn't good enough. The rules at Brad's house were very strict, and he learned when he was small that he could get out of trouble if he gave a really good reason for doing whatever he did. He got very good at making up stories that his mother would accept. It's no wonder he had difficulty telling the truth and knowing what's real.

Coming from a competitive household, Harry Hardy could remember trying to win since he was four and his seven-year-old sister ran faster than he did. When they played Chutes and Ladders when he was five, he always felt frustrated when he lost. He thought he wasn't good enough. Harry didn't know that a sister three years older had maturity on her side, and no one ever explained it to him. He felt that if he tried hard enough he could win, and if he didn't win he hadn't tried hard enough. By the time he was ten Harry was tired of trying hard and never being good enough. He decided to let go of all the trying—except in sports. Harry was a good athlete. In high school he played football, basketball, and baseball. He was in the long-jump and shot-put events on the track and field team. When he won second place in shot put at the state meet, he was disappointed in himself for not getting first.

After looking at the perfect teeth, hair, eyes, noses, mouths, and bodies on television, it's no wonder Polly, Brad, and Harry think they don't look good enough. Polly is tall and slender, but she sees herself as skinny and thinks her neck makes her look like a giraffe. Brad has a great smile, but he thinks his nose is too big and his eyes bug out. Even though he works out, he is not able to bulk up the way he would like to. He isn't very tall, so he wants to have a great body to make up for it. Having a good build is taken for granted by Harry because he's been active in sports for so long. Harry wishes his hair weren't so curly and his feet weren't so big and the braces were off his teeth. So three attractive teenagers think they are un-attractive and unappealing because they don't live up to their self-imposed critical standards of perfection. It's as though they were at the carnival fun house looking in the mirrors and believing the distortions to be reality.

Believing distortions is the rule rather than the excep-tion for most teens today. Most of the distortions were planted in your brain when you were very small and didn't know how to interpret them. When parents said, "You're a bad boy," you believed them. You didn't know how to separate your behavior from who you are. That you make mistakes does not make you a bad person. That, as a child, you used bad judgment and did things that parents, teach-ers, neighbors, grandparents, and friends didn't approve of doesn't make you a bad person. If people have been harsh with you, you may have decided that since they think you're bad, you must be bad, even though you don't know what you did that was so bad. Believing the lie of per-fection and accepting the judgments on behavior as judg-ments of worth, of good and bad, you have been looking at yourself in carnival mirrors and believing the distortion to be the real you.

It's time to look at your self-image, what you think of yourself, and see if you've been looking in a carnival mirror. If you have, your self-esteem has been taking a beating. You have allowed others to tell you who you are. The people who influenced you in the development of your self-image were doing the best they knew how to do at the time. Every human being operates on the experience and knowledge gained up to the moment of decision, and all decisions made are the best that can be made at the time. Some of the decisions you are operating on now were made at a time when your powers of evaluation and insight were limited because of your age and level of maturity. It's time to reevaluate that programming, to get a new mirror, to get rid of the lies and distortions that have ruled your life. It's time to realize that your self-esteem is really yours, and no one else is responsible for it. All you need to provide you with warm, loving feelings toward yourself is right inside of you.

You learned to look for your "feel good" from outside when you were a newborn. You cried and someone fed you. You cried and someone changed your wet diaper so you were warm and comfortable again. You couldn't dress yourself. You had to be taken outdoors and watched carefully so you would be safe. People did things to you and for you. You learned to seek comfort and good feelings from outside.

As you grew you learned that warmth and love came from your parents, and when they approved of what you did you got warm and loving feelings from them. When they disapproved, the warmth and love were replaced with anger, frustration, sadness, or other negative feelings. To keep the good feelings coming, you learned to seek your parents' approval by doing what they wanted you to do. As your world expanded and included other people—grandparents, uncles, aunts, cousins, neighbors, family friends, teachers, friends—the seeking for approval continued. Perhaps you discovered that to feel good you had to have the approval of other people. In all the approval seeking, you forgot the most important person who needs to approve of you—YOU!

When you look for your "feel good" outside of yourself by seeking approval from others, you give away your self-esteem. Self-esteem is in the self. "Other" esteem will never be enough for the self. Approval seekers can never get enough approval from others to feel good about themselves because feeling good about yourself comes from inside.

Since self-esteem comes from within, no one can give it to you, and no one can take it away. You are in charge of how you feel about yourself. The choices you make from this moment on will determine how you feel about yourself. You have the choice to feel good or bad. There may be circumstances in your life that are difficult to live with, and they may be unchangeable. Since you can't change the circumstances, change the way you think about them because your thoughts determine how you feel about yourself.

Very simply, self-esteem is how warm and loving you feel toward yourself. Your feelings about yourself come from your convictions about yourself as a capable, competent person having worth. Feeling capable is having self-confidence, viewing yourself as able to cope effectively with the challenges of life. A feeling of worth means having self-respect, which comes as a result of living up to your own standard of values. Your self-esteem is a result of your evaluation of yourself and the extent to which you believe yourself to be a capable, worthy person. It is a *personal* judgment, and it can be based on truth or distortion, on reality or imagination. Based on the truth that your worth as a human being is a birthright that no one can give or take away, that comes with your first breath of life and is yours until your last breath is taken, you are worthy of happiness and respect in this world. So face your reality: You are a worthy and important person who deserves to feel good every day of your life, and the only things keeping you from enjoying the gifts of self-confidence and self-respect are your thoughts about you and your world.

CHAPTER 2

The Choice Is Yours

Elbow on the desk and chin in his hand, Dan Dawdle looked up from his history book and stared at the wall. He could have been at the movies with his friends, but instead he had to do his homework. What a drag! Just because it was Sunday, and he had been too busy to do it Friday night or Saturday, his parents wouldn't trust him to do it after he got home from the early show. He wasn't getting much done anyway; he'd just as well have gone to the movie. It was always the same. Dan had to do his homework when he wanted to do something else. He always seemed to be stuck doing what he didn't want to do.

Take what happened last Monday. Dan was standing on the corner talking to the guys, and his mother came out of the store with a cart full of groceries. When she saw him, she waved for him to come over. She told him she'd give him a ride home and he could help her take the groceries in. He didn't want to go home yet because he had a ride with Rick Romeo. There were always lots of girls around Rick, and Dan was looking forward to cruising a while with him. Instead he rode home with his mother and carried groceries into the house.

Next week would be Thanksgiving. Holidays were really a bummer for Dan. He had to go to his grandparents' house and pretend to be interested in his aunts and uncles and all his cousins. The only one near his age was his cousin Constance, who was a year younger and always did everything right. Last year at Christmas he had been looking out the window at the decorations in the yard across the street when Constance said that he hadn't brought in wood for the fireplace. Nobody had asked him to get wood or told him it was his job. When Dan had sat down to read the sports page, he heard Constance tell Grandmother that he would go next door to borrow a card table from the neighbors. Dan never had a chance to relax because Constance would remind him of things to do or, worse yet, give Grandmother ideas of things for him to do. He was not looking forward to the family gathering next week.

As he stared at the wall, Dan felt powerless over forces that seemed to control him. Wherever he was, someone would find something for him to do that he didn't want to do. Lately even his friends were getting into the act. On Tuesday when he drove the guys to school, he told them that he wanted to leave right after school so he could apply for a job as courtesy clerk at the grocery store. They all said okay, but when Dan was ready to leave the guys were talking to girls and wouldn't leave. By the time he got to the store, the job was filled. Dan was really angry and upset about that. If he hadn't had to wait for his friends, he might have got the job. The guys knew he wanted to leave, but they didn't care about what he wanted. Dan had wanted to leave them, but since he had taken them to school, he felt obligated to wait for them. And now, tonight, he had no choice about his homework. His parents wouldn't listen to reason, so here he sat staring at the wall. It really was unfair!

Peggy Pleezer felt frustrated and angry. She was left to do all the cleaning up again. When her sister Nodda had suggested they make cookies, Peggy had agreed to do it if Nodda would help with the cleaning up. Nodda loved to bake, and when she did she made a mess of the entire kitchen. Some kind of emergency always seemed to happen for Nodda just when it was time to clean up, and Peggy was left with the mess. Even with the commitment ahead of time to stay and help, Nodda had managed to escape again, and Peggy was left holding the bag, or in this case the dirty mixing bowl. "One of these days," thought Peggy, "I'll leave the mess and let Mom see what Nodda does to the kitchen."

Cleaning the kitchen after her sister was not the only thing Peggy did that she didn't want to do. Her friends were always asking her for favors and took for granted that she would do them. They would borrow things and not return them for months. Phyllis Philch borrowed a favorite sweater, wore it several times to school, and gave it back to Peggy when it needed to be cleaned! Peggy hadn't wanted to lend Phyllis anything again, but when Bruce Brawny asked Phyllis to go to the Homecoming Dance with him, Peggy was the only one in their crowd who had a dressy handbag, so she had to lend it to Phyllis.

Teachers were always asking Peggy to do things, too. They were so pleased because she would do a job quickly and well. When Ms. Bunsun, the chemistry teacher, needed help setting up chemicals for lab days, she asked Peggy to come in before school and help her. Peggy had to take an early bus rather than getting a ride with her friends; it meant getting up at 5:30 in the morning. Peggy wished Ms. Bunsun would ask someone else because she hated to get up so early. It seemed unfair to Peggy to be the only one asked to help.

Ms. Bunsen wasn't the only one who asked Peggy to do things outside of school time. Mr. Swift, the track coach, asked her to time the practice races the team had once a week, so on Thursdays all spring Peggy didn't get home from school until 5:30 or 6:00. Last year she had been interested in Harry Hardy and had been glad to stay every week. This year she wasn't interested in anyone on the track team, but she didn't want to let Coach Swift down so she had agreed to be his timer on Thursdays. What else could she do?

Dan and Peggy weren't the only ones feeling trapped into doing things they didn't want to do. Dan didn't know it but his grandmother, Dona Dawdle, really didn't want to cook Thanksgiving dinner! She wished one of her daughters-in-law would take on that responsibility. Getting all the china, crystal, and silver ready for a big family dinner was becoming a big job for her, to say nothing of the preparation of the turkey and dressing. Family members brought the rest of the meal and helped prepare it, but she still had more to do than she wanted. Even though her daughters-in-law cleaned up after dinner, they didn't put things away in the right places, and Dona still had to clean up the house after everyone left. She was dreading the work of another Thanksgiving and Christmas. Having all the children there at one time was so hard on her nerves. She longed for no responsibility during the holidays, but of course she couldn't tell her family that. She would manage somehow, but she felt weighed down with the thought.

Meanwhile, back in the chemistry lab, Ms. Bunsun was having difficulties of her own, but they didn't have to do with chemistry. She had agreed to go out with the man in the apartment next door because he had said he was new to the area and didn't know anyone and she had felt sorry for him. Now she was feeling sorry for herself because she didn't want to go out with him. They had talked in the hall the other night, and Ms. Bunsun thought he was tiresome and boring. All he could talk about was computers, and she wasn't interested. She was disgusted with herself for saying she would go out with the guy, but she didn't see any way out of it. Just thinking about it made her more frustrated.

Have To or Choose To?

When you do things you don't want to do you usually feel angry, frustrated, trapped, obligated, and disgusted. You feel pushed around and don't feel good about yourself. It's as though you're saying, "I'm the one who has to do this, but I didn't choose it." The cause of all your bad feeling is not that you are doing what you don't want to do, but that you are doing what you *think* you don't want to do. Ms. Bunsun is going out with her neighbor because she *thinks* she has no choice. Peggy is cleaning the kitchen because she *thinks* she has no choice. Dan is doing his homework because he *thinks* he has no choice. Dona is going to cook Thanksgiving dinner because she *thinks* she has no choice. Actually, they all made the choice to do what they did.

Unfortunately, most people believe that "want = enjoy" and "choose = like," so if they don't like or enjoy something, they think they didn't choose it. What would happen if Ms. Bunsun told her neighbor she didn't want to go out with him? She thinks he would be disappointed. She thinks he might be angry and think she is a terrible person. She thinks he might tell all her neighbors how she treated him—on second thought, he would probably be too embarrassed to tell anyone. She thinks of so many negative things that might happen if she doesn't go out with him that she chooses to keep the date because of the emotional pain to her and her neighbor if she were to break it. She doesn't like her choice. She doesn't enjoy her choice. But it *is* her choice.

In the matter of homework, Dan had several choices. He could have done it Friday afternoon as soon as he got home from school or on Saturday. However, he chose to put it off until the last possible moment. Even though his parents told him to get it done, Dan still had the choice of refusing to do it. He felt that the consequences of defying his parents would make that a bad choice, so he chose to do the homework. He has to go through the motions of getting the work done to satisfy his parents; however, the consequences of not doing it at all would be a low grade that would be unacceptable to his parents. Doing his homework, even though he didn't like or enjoy it, was Dan's choice for Sunday evening because the consequences of not doing it were more painful.

Feeling trapped by family tradition, Dona Dawdle feels she has no choice but to cook the turkey for Thanksgiving. What would happen if she told the family that she would rather not do it this year? Dona thinks they would all be disappointed, that her daughters-in-law would feel obligated to fill in for her, that the family would think there was something wrong with her, that her sons would be angry. The Voice in Dona's head can give her a dozen reasons why she *should* cook for Thanksgiving, why she *has* to cook. Consequently, she decided to cook.

The choice you make is always the best choice you can make at the time you are making it. Dan, Ms. Bunsun, and Dona chose to do what seemed to be the best thing to do at the time. They didn't like it or enjoy it, so they said to themselves, "I'm the one who has to do it, but I didn't choose it." That kind of thinking keeps you feeling like a victim. Someone or something is "doing it" to you because you don't like or enjoy it.

To get out of your "victim thinking," you must look at choice-making a little differently. If you were asked to choose between a vacation in Maui or a vacation in London, which would you choose? If you had to choose between $500 cash or a diamond ring, which would you choose? If you could have an A on your report card or a week out of class, which would you choose? Suppose you had to choose between walking one mile home or waiting alone for three hours for a ride? What if your choice were between cleaning the garage for your dad or mopping the floor for your mom? Which would you choose, going without breakfast or going without dinner? When the choice is between two positive things, you can make a clear choice very easily—I want $500. When the choice is between two negatives, it becomes a little sticky, but given the choice, you choose the one that has the least amount of "feel bad" to it at the time. If it's raining outside, you would probably be willing to wait three hours rather than walk a mile in the rain. However, you would very likely be angry about it and say that you had no choice. Most of the time if it's a choice between "bad" and "worse," you'll get rid of "worse" and say you didn't choose "bad."

When the choice is between two things you don't like or enjoy, you fail to see that you've made a choice. Peggy felt Nodda was taking advantage of her and resented having to clean the kitchen. Peggy chose to clean the kitchen rather than face her mother's disapproval. Hassling with her mother about the messy kitchen was worse than cleaning up the mess herself. She chose what provided the least amount of "feel bad" at that moment. However, she blamed her sister for her bad feelings about what she chose to do because she didn't see it as her own choice.

When you begin to see that whatever you do is what you choose even if you don't like or enjoy it, you will be able to look for other options from which to choose. What options does Peggy have besides the one she chose? She could choose not to bake cookies with Nodda. She could speak to her mother about getting stuck with a mess and work out an arrangement so that the mess could be left for Nodda to clean up later. She could scream at Nodda and tell her what a jerk she is. (Probably not a very productive idea, but it *is* an option.) She could deal with Nodda assertively instead of saying nothing and feeling resentful or fighting with her about it. When you look at options, you begin to see that you are not powerless. You do have control over the choices in your life, and options give you power.

You are most likely to make choices you don't like when you are not willing to take the emotional consequences of choosing differently. Ms. Bunsun was afraid that the man next door might think she was terrible, that he wouldn't like her, so her fear of rejection caused her to do what she thought she didn't want to do. Besides that, he would be disappointed so she felt obligated to go out with him, and she had some fleeting feelings of guilt when she thought he might tell someone else. The emotional cost seemed so high that Ms. Bunsun chose what she felt would give her the least amount of pain.

Many times your choice are made because you don't want to go outside of your comfort zone. The thought of telling her family that she did not want to cook Thanksgiving dinner made Dona feel very uncomfortable. She didn't think they would approve of her not wanting to cook. She did not know how to tell them how she felt without feeling guilty. To express her true feelings was outside of her comfort zone. In every case, Peggy, Dan, Ms. Bunsun, and Dona, they didn't feel that their feelings were as valuable as the feelings of others. They didn't have the self-confidence to express their true feelings. In a word, they were all nonassertive. They were unwilling to move out of their comfort zone, to risk the possibility of someone else's disapproval. Thus they kept themselves victims by think-ing they had no choice.

If you have thought in the past that you had to do things you didn't want to do because you had no choice, it's time to own up to the truth. Everything you do, you do because it is the best choice you can make at the time. You may not like or enjoy it, but you're the one who chooses. Whatever you think will give you the most "feel good" and the least "feel bad" at the time is what you will choose. You are in charge of your life and always have been. You'll feel very different about what goes on in your life when you accept that you do have choices. If you are doing things you feel you don't want to do, you can learn ways to deal with the inner Voice that says you "shouldn't" do this or you "can't" do that or asks you, "What will people think?" You can learn to go outside your comfort zone and take risks so that you can gain the self-confidence to make choices that are better for you long range. The choice is yours.

CHAPTER ◇ 3

Where Is Your
Self-Worth?

As she walked down the hall, Ava Rishus looked enviously at Debi Dapper's new dress. Debi had everything—clothes, car, boyfriend, and especially money. Her parents gave her anything she wanted and plenty that she didn't even ask for. Debi wore all the latest styles and must have had forty pairs of shoes and untold numbers of belts, bags, and jewelry. Smiling and happy, popular, with lots of friends, Debi had everything that Ava wanted. Ava was sure that she would be as happy and popular as Debi if she had the money to buy clothes like Debi's and had parents who gave her anything she wanted and let her go anywhere she wanted. Everybody would like her, and she wouldn't have a care in the world.

Walking not far behind Ava was Mark Merit. Mark was in a hurry to get to his locker and pick up the committee list for the band yard sale. He would need the list for the meeting at lunch. He was the band representative on the board of the parents' Band Boosters Club, and it was his responsibility to organize the committees from the band who would be working with the parents and gathering the stuff for the sale. Mark didn't mind doing the job, but he couldn't waste any time because he had so many other things to do.

Besides being in the band, Mark had a 3.7 grade point average, was on the varsity basketball team, wrote a column for the school newspaper, and had a part-time job at a fast-food restaurant. He also was a volunteer at the convalescent hospital near his home the first Saturday afternoon of each month. People were always amazed at how much he was involved in and how much he accomplished. Mark was a real "doer."

With his backpack full of books over one shoulder, Walt Wisdom said hi to Mark as they passed in the hall. Walt was a very serious student. He knew that if he wanted to be successful in life he had to have a good education. He wanted to go to a private university so he could get the best possible education, and he hoped to get a scholarship that would take care of most of the tuition. He already knew that he would not be satisfied with a bachelor's degree and was planning what he would study in graduate school.

The importance of education was constantly emphasized in Walt's home. His father had gone to work right after high school, unable to go to college because his income was needed to help his mother feed the family. Mr. Wisdom had felt the lack of education all his life. He was sure that if he'd had the opportunity to go to college he would have been a professional man and would have been able to do much more for his family. Walt sensed how important education was to his parents and also felt their sense of lack because neither had gone to college. His dad was always telling him to study hard so he would know more than his "old man."

As Walt turned to go into his history class, he almost bumped into Felicia Fetching, who was hurrying out. Felicia wasn't watching where she was going because she had her head down to hide the tears in her eyes. She wished she could leave this school and never come back. After six weeks at the school she didn't have any friends, and now this. As she was gathering up her books to leave class, she overheard part of a conversation between Rudy Goash and Sherman Sharp. Rudy was looking in Felicia's direction and said something about zits and braces being bad enough. She knew what the rest of the conversation was about—her weight.

Although her mother told her she wasn't fat, Felicia knew she was. She hated to dress in P.E., not only because she looked so ugly in shorts, but also because she didn't want anyone to see how fat she was with her clothes off. Her thighs looked like cottage cheese, they had so much cellulite! Wearing long, loose shirts and sweaters with pants and skirts helped cover up some of the ugliness, but Felicia was sure that everyone could see how fat she was anyway.

The part about the zits and braces had been really cruel, Felicia thought. Lots of kids had braces and nobody thought too much about them. Wearing braces had never been important before, but Rudy made it sound like a big defect, and the comment about zits really hurt. Felicia had been going to a dermatologist for two years, and her face was doing much better. She faithfully did everything the doctor told her to do. Why, she had thought this morning that her face looked almost clear, and then Rudy had to remind her that it was still a mess. If only she had clear skin and were cute and petite like Polly Perfect! Then she would have lots of friends.

Coming out of the classroom right behind Felicia was

Steve Strain. Steve was as upset as Felicia because he had heard all of what Rudy was saying to Sherm, and it was about him, not Felicia. The rest of the sentence had been, "but to take a girl to a dance with your father driving the car is too much!" Steve and Connie Jeanial had been friends since first grade. They decided to go to the Homecoming dance together since neither had a date, and they didn't consider it a big deal. When Steve's dad offered to give them a ride since neither had a driver's license, they thought it was a great idea. In fact, they had gone out to dinner with Steve's parents before the dance. At the time it seemed like an okay thing to do, and he and Connie had a good time. When he heard Rudy, however, Steve began to feel real uncomfortable about it. This was an example of what happened to him all the time. He would think something was all right and find out that others thought it was weird.

Some of the things Steve thought were fun to do he had stopped doing, because others thought there was something wrong with him when he did them. One day he was swinging on a swing at the little kids' playground because he had always liked to swing, and two guys from school saw him and gave him a bad time. He'd passed on the swings since then. Another time Steve had mentioned something about the school choir, and Brad Brasher had made a comment about wimps being in the choir. Steve had decided to pass on joining the choir. When he went to try out for the school play, he found out that he would have to dance, and he knew what the guys would think about that so he passed on the school play.

Sometimes Steve got stuck doing things he didn't want to do because he was afraid someone would think he wasn't a good guy if he said no. When Ima Imposer asked to borrow his history notes to study for a test, Steve really did not want to let her use them, but he was afraid she would think he was selfish so he lent her the notes. When Ima returned them, Harry Hardy had been with him, and Harry told Steve he was crazy to lend Ima his notes. So Steve ended up wrong anyway.

On Tuesday when he was leaving for school, his mother had stopped him at the door and made him change his shirt because a button was missing, saying, "What will people think if they see you wearing a shirt with a button missing?" He hadn't thought much about it until then, but he guessed they'd think he was a slob so he had changed his shirt. Steve was beginning to think that no matter what he did or how hard he tried, someone was bound to think that he was wrong.

WHERE IS YOUR WORTH?

Your Worth Is Not in What You Have

Since she didn't feel good about herself, Ava Rishus looked at others who looked as though they felt good and she wanted what they had. Ava was sure that Debi Dapper was happy and popular because she had so many "things," and Ava thought she could feel good if she had the things that Debi had. She even wished she could have Debi's parents because she saw them as providing more material things and personal freedom for Debi. Ava was way off track with her thinking. No "things" that she had ever had made her feel good for very long.

When she was in sixth grade Ava had felt left out because all the girls were wearing Calvin Klein jeans and she didn't have any. She hassled her mother until she got the jeans. When she got to school with her Calvin Klein jeans on, nobody was any more friendly to her than they had been before. It wasn't two weeks until Ava was sure that what she needed to feel good and accepted was a new jacket like the one Trisha Trendy had. When no amount of hassling got the jacket because her father absolutely refused to spend that much money on something Ava didn't even need, Ava was sure she would never be accepted by her peers, and it was all her parents' fault.

One of the happiest people in eighth grade had been Jennifer Jentry. Jenni wasn't terribly cute and she didn't have especially nice clothes, but she did have a good-looking boyfriend. Ava figured that she was as cute as Jenni and dressed even better, so it must have been the boy-friend who was making Jenni so happy. If only she could have Jenni's boyfriend, Ava was sure she would feel good about herself. So Ava went on a campaign to get Jenni's boyfriend, and she did; however, her happiness lasted less than three weeks. He was good-looking all right, but he expected Ava to make him happy, and she expected him to make her happy. Between the two of them, no one was happy.

It seemed that no matter what Ava got, it never made her happy for long, so she was always looking for something to make her feel good. She was always wondering why people didn't like her and never stopped to think of the dead bodies she left along the way. Jenni was not the only one who suffered from Ava's search for self-worth.

Somewhere along the way Ava had accepted the lie that your self-worth lies in what you have. All the commercials on TV tell you that you'll be happy if. . .you have a new, imported Super Turbo 850 XZ; you use Shino Toothpaste and get the beautiful girl beside the pool; you have new carpet, new shoes, new appliances. Magazines tell you that you can have the woman/man of your dreams if you drink the right booze, smoke the right cigarette, drive the right car, wear the right clothes. The natural conclusion to draw is that the way to happiness and feeling good about yourself is through what you have. That is a lie! The way to happiness and feeling good is through who you are, not what you have.

When what you have is never enough, you know you have bought the lie. The right jeans didn't make Ava happy, nor did the right boyfriend. The right parents or having money won't make her feel good about herself either. Nothing outside herself will make Ava feel good about herself because self-worth is not in what you have but in who you are.

Your Self-worth Is Not in What You Do

Mark Merit bought the lie that your self-worth is in what you do. Sometime in his early years he connected his self-worth to his behavior. Mark got lots of praise for helping around the house, being a good student, being responsible, and being involved in school activities. He thought that the more he could do, the better he would feel. Completing the job, running the committee, getting the highest grade on the test were ways that Mark could see his accomplishments. Funny thing about it, he never felt that he had done enough. It always seemed that he could have done more, better, in less time.

When your self-worth is tied up in what you do, you are always judging yourself. Your critical judge, the Voice in your head, constantly tells you that you have not done anything as well as it could be done. Even when others tell you what a wonderful job you've done, the Voice tells you that you could have done it better. It seems that no matter how much you do, the Voice is always pushing you on because there is no such thing as "enough"—good enough, fast enough, perfect enough, thorough enough. The Voice tells you that you aren't trying hard enough, that you aren't doing enough. Because nothing is enough, you feel inadequate. You've bought the lie that your worth is in what you do.

People who believe their worth is in what they do feel that they have to be perfect or else they are bad. They don't allow themselves to be human and make mistakes. Errors in judgment become a chance for the Voice to scold and punish. "You really messed up this time!" "When will you ever learn?" "How could you have done something so stupid?" "You deserve to lose the starting spot." With the self-punishment come the feelings of inadequacy and low self-esteem that throw you into wanting to *do* something if you are a "doer."

Some people who believe their worth is in what they do were told as children that they were bad when they did something wrong—not that what they *did* was bad, but that *they* were bad. Some children who are severely punished or abused by parents grow up believing that they are bad because, even though they don't know what they did that was so bad, they feel they must be bad or they wouldn't have been so mistreated. Their belief often is, "I must be perfect or I'm bad, so since I can't be perfect, I won't do anything," or, "Since I'm always in trouble no matter how hard I try, I might just as well do something bad because I'm no good anyway." A third attitude is, "Maybe if I try really hard to be good, they'll notice and tell me how good I am." Unfortunately, "they" are never satisfied, the person is never good enough, and the feelings of being a bad person are reinforced. All three responses are very sad and very incorrect because your worth is not in what you do.

Mark Merit believed that he had to be doing something all the time or there was something wrong with him. People who believe as Mark believed have a Voice in their head that says, "Don't waste time. You must be doing something productive with your time." The Voice never lets them rest and relax. They don't know how to do nothing. They feel that they are judged by what they do—how much, how well, and how fast. They never do a job well enough or soon enough, and they are convinced by the Voice that they could have done more. They don't know how to set limits and take time for themselves.

Our society encourages this kind of thinking. The American way is to do the job better and faster. If a little is good, then more must be better. If a twenty-story building is an accomplishment, then let's build one with thirty and be better. If you can type forty words a minute, you are better than someone who can only type thirty but not as good as someone who can type fifty. Somehow in all this doing it better your self-esteem gets involved. It may be difficult for you to separate what you do from who you are. If you're the person who types thirty words per minute, you may believe that you are not as worthy as those who type fifty. Harry Hardy's self-worth was so tied up in what he did that the truly superb accomplishment of coming in second in a state track meet was disregarded because he didn't come in first, and he felt "less than," not good enough.

If you feel in a hurry all the time and that no matter how much you do you just don't measure up to your expectations or the expectations of others, you are being controlled by the false belief that your worth is in what you do. The truth is that your worth is in who you are. As a human being you have infinite worth; no matter what you do or don't do, you are worthy and important.

Your Self-worth Is Not in What You Know

In this world of constantly changing and developing technology, education is extremely important and college degrees are commonplace. It seems that advanced degrees are becoming more and more necessary. As more emphasis is put on knowledge and learning, people are getting what they know confused with who they are. Walt Wisdom's father had felt "less than" all his life because he didn't have a college education. He did not think he was as important or worthy as those who had gone to college. Walt was programmed from an early age to work hard so he could go to college. He bought the lie from his father and others in our society that your worth is in what you know.

Walt was always striving for the next academic accomplishment, the next educational hurdle. He was looking to future knowledge to make him feel good. The more he learned, the surer he was sure that the next goal reached would make him feel adequate. When Walt gets his Ph.D. after years of graduate school, he will still be trying to be adequate because he believes his worth is in what he knows instead of in who he is.

If you have a brother or sister who is a high achiever at school, and you are not, you may feel "less than" and inadequate. You may be putting down your special talents because you are not an academic high achiever. You may be a "people" person and excel in working and getting along with others. Corinne Cordial worked hard to get Cs in school, yet she felt she was letting her parents down. She was talking to Ms. Guide, her counselor, one day, and Ms. Guide suggested that Corinne take an after-school job at the day-care center down the street. When she began working with the children at the day-care center, Corinne found that she loved being with them, and the director thought she was wonderful. It wasn't long until the director called Corinne's parents to tell them how much she appreciated their daughter and what a wonderful addition she was to the day-care program. Corinne began to appreciate her special talents and see herself as successful, even though she was not academically talented.

Allan Apt had so much difficulty learning to read that he thought he was the dumbest person in the world. However, when he was in fifth grade, his teacher, Mr. Alert, noticed how Allan could take things apart and put them back together. Allan had been getting in trouble for years for "fiddling" with things. At first he hadn't always got them back together properly, but after a while he became very good at it so his parents didn't know he had been "fiddling" with them. Mr. Alert recognized Allan's talent and encouraged him to create new things from some old gadgets that had been lying around the Alerts' garage. That started Allan on a wonderful, creative adventure, and now in his senior year in high school he was designing the lighting for the summer outdoor stage production of the school's community theater. It was still a struggle to read and keep up with his school work, but Allan hadn't felt stupid since fifth grade.

If you're always going after the grade and when you get it feel that it isn't enough, if getting a lower grade than you expected, even if it's a B, is like failing, if you can't enjoy getting the highest grade in the class on the test because your Voice tells you that you could have done better, you have probably swallowed the lie that your worth is in what you know. You've been walking up the steps to get to where it feels good, but you've been taking the wrong staircase. Your worth is in who you are, and you don't have to know anything more than that. The contribution you make to the world is the gift of yourself. Knowing who you are and appreciating you is the most important bit of learning you can master! Strive for the best you can do with the talents you have. If you are academically talented, make the most of that talent and don't allow your Voice to put you down for not being perfect. If you have talents in other areas, enjoy those special talents and don't allow the Voice to put you down by telling you that you aren't smart in school so you're a dumb person. Your self-worth is in who you are.

Your Self-worth Is Not in Your Physical Appearance

In our society great importance is put on how you look. Political figures who do not look well on TV might as well not start the race. Christine Craft, a TV newswoman, won a nationally publicized lawsuit against a TV station that fired her because they said she wasn't attractive enough to be their anchorperson. Model/actress Lauren Hutton has a gap between her front teeth and often wears a filler when she goes on modeling assignments so her teeth will appear perfect. Beauty products abound for every possible physical shortcoming—from dull, lifeless hair to poor posture. If you are less than perfect in any respect, there must be a pill, powder, lotion, cream, foam, exercise, gadget, gismo, or doodad that will fix it. The implication is that if you are less than perfect, there's something wrong with you.

When you're young and growing, your body doesn't always do what you would like it to do. Being short for a boy can be very painful, and growing tall at early age can be equally painful for a girl. Retaining the softer, rounder look of a child causes grief and suffering when everyone else is developing a more mature physique. Those with curly hair wish it were straight, and people with straight hair envy those whose hair is curly. If you like your nose, you probably wish you had prettier eyes. If you have a great smile, you no doubt think your ears are too big.

Weight is of major importance to many people regardless of age. Being overweight is almost a crime, and what is considered overweight in themselves by teenagers would be perfection for their mothers! If a teen does happen to be overweight, it seems that few look beyond that to the person. Many are like Felicia Fetching, who was sure that anyone who whispered and looked in her direction was talking about how fat she was. There were many attractive things about her, but it was difficult for people to get to know her and find out what kind of person she was. She had built a wall around herself because she was so sensitive about her weight. She didn't realize that she was keeping people out. She was so sure she would be rejected by others that she rejected them first. She was sure that her worth was in her appearance, and since her appearance was so unacceptable to her, the Voice in her head told her that she was unacceptable to others.

Many young women have believed the lie about worth being in appearance and have become ill trying not to be fat. Anorexia and bulimia are commonplace in our society. If the Voice in your head is telling you that you are fat and you can't eat for fear of gaining weight while everyone else tells you that you are too thin; if you can never lose enough weight to satisfy yourself, you may have slipped into anorexia. If you eat and then make yourself vomit or take laxatives so the food won't stay in your body long enough to cause you to gain weight, you're practicing bulimia. Both anorexia and bulimia produce the same end result— starvation.

Accepting who you are and how you look is difficult for most Americans. Women of forty want to look like Jane Fonda and girls as young as ten wish they looked like

Madonna. There's an ideal for everyone. Young men want bodies like Sylvester Stallone or to look like Tom Cruise. If they like the Don Johnson look, they'll feel bad because they could never have his five o'clock shadow even if they didn't shave for a month!

Pimples have been the curse of young people since time began. In our perfectionist society, zits can seem like a terminal illness. Some young people, like Felicia, are able to see a dermatologist and have their acne treated. Others are not fortunate enough to have the insurance coverage, the money, or the parental understanding to get treatment. Believing their worth is in their appearance, having zits makes them feel "less than."

Wearing the right clothes and having your hair cut the right way are vital to your self-esteem if you believe that your worth is in your appearance. When you look right, if the Voice in your head is still telling you that you aren't okay, you're finding out that your worth is not in your appearance. No matter how you look, there will be something about you that the Voice thinks could be better. It is leading you to believe the lie that your worth is in your appearance, while the truth is that your worth is in who you are.

Your Worth Is Not in What Other People Think

Just because someone else says something doesn't make it true, but Steve Strain believed that it did. He and Connie had a good time together at the Homecoming dance, but he allowed what someone else thought to change how he felt about the evening. Steve was often confused by what he thought was okay and what he found out other people thought. What other people think is none of your business!

If someone tells you that you can't walk on the sidewalk in front of the post office, do you say, "Thanks for the information," and never step on the sidewalk in front of the post office? The next time you want to buy stamps or mail a package, you walk on the sidewalk in front of the post office, go in the door, and take care of your business. It doesn't matter if someone else thinks you can't walk on the sidewalk in front of the post office! What other people think is none of your business!

What other people think can't hurt you unless you let it. Try this little experiment. When someone doesn't know you are observing them, for ten seconds think all of the positive thoughts that you can about them, just keep positive ideas about them in your mind. Then for ten seconds think only negative thoughts about them. Call them names and think all the stupid, ugly things you can about them. Watch them very closely while you think your positive and then negative thoughts. Did you notice how happy and delighted they looked while you were thinking the positive thoughts and how devastated they were by your negative thoughts? Now you know the importance of what other people think.

What is important is what *you* think. You may be like Steve if you've been into what other people think. Steve didn't know what *he* thought because he was so busy trying to fit what other people thought. It's time for you to spend some time with yourself deciding what's important to you. If you like to sing, it's none of your business what other people think about boys who are in the choir.

If you truly believe that dissection is wrong, then you will tell your counselor that you have a problem with lab sciences that require dissection. If the counselor tries to talk you out of your convictions, you may need to get help from your parents in dealing with the situation. What *you* think is what is important, and what the counselor thinks is none of your business.

In the fall of 1986 a young man in Elk Grove, California, decided to run for Homecoming "King." He was very serious in his candidacy and felt it would be a fun thing to be a part of. He did not think the contest should be limited to girls, and nothing in the policy governing the contest said it was for girls only. His parents and many of his fellow students supported him. It created quite a stir and the school administration declared him ineligible for the contest and asked him to withdraw. The young man agreed to withdraw when the administration agreed to open the contest to boys in 1987. What other people thought was none of this young man's business. What *he* thought was his business.

Your worth is not in what other people think of you. Your worth is in what *you* think of you. Your self-worth is in who you are.

Where Is Your Self-worth?

When you believe the lie that your self-worth is outside of yourself—in what you do, in what you have, in what others think, in your appearance, in what you know—you are dependent on others for your happiness and warm and loving feelings toward yourself. That old idea from babyhood that others must provide you with your "feel good" is keeping you hooked into your immature emotion of needing others to make you feel good.

When you were maturing physically, you learned to take care of yourself physically. When you were five years old and hungry and your mother wasn't around, you knew where the bread and peanut butter were and managed to put the two together. You learned to tie your shoes and blow your nose. You know today that if you need clean clothes you're able to run a washing machine and dryer and take care of yourself. You may not choose to do your laundry, but you're able to learn to do it. You don't need to depend on anyone else to care for you physically.

Unfortunately, most people aren't taught how to grow up emotionally. You have been conditioned to look outside yourself for your emotional "feel good," and you still believe that your good feelings about yourself come from outside. It's as though you're walking around with a cord with a plug on it, looking for a place to plug in so you can "light up" and feel good. You carry your cord from place to place saying, "Maybe if I do that, I'll feel good. Maybe if I have that, I'll feel good. Maybe if I know that, I'll feel good. Maybe if she thinks I'm okay, I'll feel good. Maybe if I lose ten pounds, I'll feel good." You're looking to plug into happiness, but there's no "happiness plug."

There's no happiness plug because you aren't disconnected from the source of your happiness. You are one with the source. In *Star Wars* they called it the Force, and the Force was available to anyone. It was the power of the universe and was within each person. The source of self-worth, importance, and happiness is within you.

If you're thinking, "I'll be happy when...I graduate; I have enough money to enjoy myself; my parents leave me alone; I have a girlfriend who understands me; I have an apartment of my own; I have a good job," you believe that joy is in the destination; that when you get there, you'll be happy. In this life joy is in the living and you're the source of your own joy. You don't need to plug into a power source because you're battery-powered and self-charging.

CHAPTER 4

Who Has the Power to Make You Feel Bad?

After all her hard work studying the assigned chapters in the book, Greta Grumper was sure she had failed the zoology test because of stupid Ms. Fauna. The whole test was on lecture notes. Last time she had studied lecture notes and the test had been on the book! She wished Ms. Fauna would make up her mind. Teachers who did that made Greta so mad.

Mr. Zero was another one who could get Greta steamed up in no time. He was constantly complaining about people who didn't listen when he explained the algebra assignment, but he was so boring it was hard to listen to him. Besides that, he made everything more complicated than it was. When she needed help, Greta hated to ask Mr. Zero because he would accuse her of not listening. One of these days when he made her mad, she was going to tell him what she thought of him.

Although she took the same zoology test that Greta took, Melissa Meek looked at it differently. Having studied the book and lecture notes, Missie was as prepared as she could be for the test, but she felt inadequate. It seemed to her that no matter how hard she studied, she still couldn't remember enough to do very well on the test. Her mother told her that she "just didn't put her mind to it." She felt so guilty for letting everyone down. Missie knew that Ms. Fauna expected her to do well, and of course her mother expected much more of her.

It wasn't that her mother *said* she expected more of Missie, but when she took her report card home with Bs and Cs, her mother would give her a funny look as she said, "That's nice, dear," and Missie knew it wasn't nice at all. It made her feel bad when her mother did that because she tried hard to do her best.

When there were things to do around the house, Missie would try to do them the way her mother wanted them done, but she never seemed to be able to do anything right. If she did the dishes and cleaned the sink, her mother would comment that the floor could use scrubbing. The next time Missie cleaned the kitchen she would scrub the floor, and her mother would say that the dishwasher needed to be emptied. No matter what she did, there was always something she forgot, and she would have a feeling of guilt and inadequacy. Her mother didn't complain or hassle; she just looked that "Why does this have to happen to me?" look and spoke in that "I guess I can't expect everything" tone. Poor Missie wished her mother would yell and have a fit so she could complain about having an unreasonable mother.

• • •

Walking down the hall at school was agony for Patrick Pushover. Kevin Kombat had been on his case for the past week, and Patrick didn't know what to do. Whenever Kevin saw Patrick at school, he would say, "Later, Pat," in a threatening way and then smile a mean smile. He didn't do anything else, but every time he saw Patrick he would say the same thing. Patrick was really upset. He didn't think Kevin would actually hurt him. He thought Kevin was just being a bully, but he didn't know what to do about it so he tried to avoid Kevin. However, it seemed to Patrick that Kevin was making a point of finding him, and it kept him feeling constantly anxious.

Taking a deep breath and walking quickly out of the living room, Art Affable could hear the Voice in his head saying, "You shouldn't let that bother you. Don't get mad just because you don't get your way." Art could feel his heart beating as he swallowed his anger. His perfect sister Annie always got the car because she had more important things to do than he did. Why should taking her friends to the basketball game be more important than his taking his friends to the game? "She's a senior and you're a sophomore" was not good enough for him. She always won out on seniority.

It was not fair, but Art knew better than to make a big deal out of it. If his parents knew how angry he felt, they would be all over him. They made him so mad, though. He knew he shouldn't get so mad, but they always took his sister's side in everything. Art really didn't want to feel so angry all the time, but he couldn't help it. It wasn't fair!

As she walked into the insurance office where she worked, Stephanie Stable saw the little boy pull the plastic bat out of the bag his mother had put on the floor, and as he turned with the bat in his hand, he knocked over a small plant on the table. The mother jerked the bat out of the boy's hand, grabbed his arm, shook him, and growled through clenched teeth, "Now, look what you've done! I told you to leave the bat alone. Why can't you ever do what I tell you to do? Go outside and stand by the door until I come out, and just forget about getting an ice cream cone!"

The little boy looked scared and as if he wanted to cry but didn't dare. Stephanie felt so sorry for him. He hadn't meant to knock the plant over. He must have felt bad enough without his mother being so mean to him. Feeling angry toward the mother, Stephanie went over to pick up the plant, and the mother began to apologize to Stephanie's boss, saying how sorry she was that her son was so clumsy. Stephanie wanted to tell her that little boys have accidents and mothers should be understanding and not embarrass and scare them.

When she went into the back room to get the broom, Stephanie was really upset. She hated it when mothers treated their children so uncaringly. That poor little boy looked so humiliated. He had walked out with his head down and his feet dragging. The incident had spoiled Stephanie's whole day. She knew she wouldn't be able to put it out of her mind.

Who Controls Your Feelings?

Feeling angry, guilty, anxious, and scared is not fun. Those are feelings that most people don't want to feel. When you feel angry or upset, you want to look for what caused your anger and blame the person who caused it. Greta was angry and blamed Ms. Fauna and Mr. Zero for making her angry. Art's parents and sister made him angry. Stephanie was very upset because of the incident involving the little boy and the plant. The anxiety Patrick felt was caused by Kevin Kombat, and Missie's feelings of inadequacy were created by her mother's reactions.

Were all those people feeling those uncomfortable feelings because other people were "making" them feel bad? Do other people have the power to make you feel bad? Only you have the power to make you feel bad. The choice to feel good or bad is always yours.

Whether you will feel good or bad is determined by your expectations. Greta expected the test to be on the book, and she was disappointed and angry when it was on the lectures. Ms. Fauna didn't make Greta angry. Greta made Greta angry when her expectations were not met. Every time Art wanted the car and his sister got it, his expectations were not met and he was disappointed and angry. He set himself up to be angry by expecting things "to be different this time."

In every relationship you have in life, you have expectations. Your expectations are based on your past experience—how people usually act or what they usually say—and what you think someone's behavior should be. Stephanie Stable thought that a good mother should be understanding and caring. Greta Grumper thought that good teachers should explain new concepts clearly. Patrick Pushover thought that good people don't intimidate others. You have your idea of what a good friend does, what a good mother does, what a brother is supposed to do, how a father should treat a son, how a policeman behaves, what a grocery clerk does, what a good doctor is like, what a good "whatever" does. Your expectation of a good "whatever" may have nothing to do with what is actually going on.

In Art Affable's mind, parents ought to be fair. No

matter how often his parents were unfair, Art still thought that they ought to be fair. His expectation of his parents had nothing to do with what was actually going on. In Art's mind something was wrong with his parents. There's no need to judge who was right or who was wrong. Art had an expectation that was unrealistic, and his anger was a result of expecting something from his parents that was not real. His parents weren't "making him mad." Art chose to be angry when his expectation wasn't met.

As strange as it may seem, Patrick Pushover chose to feel anxious. Kevin knew that Patrick was afraid, and once he had that power over Patrick, Kevin ran with it. It was Patrick who gave Kevin the power. The Voice in Patrick's head said, "This is scary. You can't handle this," and Patrick started feeling anxious. He tried to avoid Kevin, but even in the avoidance he was giving Kevin power over his feelings. Kevin didn't make Patrick feel anxious; Patrick chose to feel anxious rather than to feel capable of handling the situation.

When you have expectations of people and situations, it's as though you are holding an invisible sign that says, "In order for me to feel okay, you have to. . ." That would be fine if others could read your sign. Unfortunately, you expect (another expectation!) them to know what the sign says even though they can't *see* the sign! Patrick is walking around with his sign saying, "Kevin, in order for me to feel good, you have to stop trying to intimidate me." One of Greta's signs says, "In order for me to feel okay, Mr. Zero, you have to be patient with me when I ask you questions about what you have just explained." For her mother, Missie Meek has a sign that says, "Mom, if I'm going to feel okay, you have to accept me as I am and not expect more than I can give."

Since you're the only one who knows what's on your

sign, take a look and see what you're carrying around. The caption on your sign always starts. "For me to feel okay, you have to. . ." When the other person doesn't make you feel okay, you are very likely to say, "What's wrong with you?" Mr. Zero was an unreasonable grouch; Art's parents were unfair; Kevin was a bully. If you expect your friend to be on time and she's late, you can get angry and call her inconsiderate. When your mother won't let you leave until the dishes are done and the kitchen is cleaned, you can be angry and say she's hard-hearted. You're saying that it's her fault you feel bad because she won't do what you want her to do (let you leave without doing the dishes) so you won't feel angry and resentful.

By making the other person wrong, you feel a sense of justification in your bad feelings. You can tell your sad story to others who will agree that the other person is wrong, but it won't change what's happening. Who's holding the sign? Who's feeling bad? Kevin doesn't feel bad because Patrick thinks he's a bully. Mr. Zero isn't upset because Greta won't ask him to explain an assignment to her. Who's stuck feeling bad? *The person holding the sign!* What's producing the anger, fear, or guilt? *The unrealistic expectation that is not being met.*

When you hold on to an expectation and reject reality, it's like kicking a brick wall, expecting to get through it and wondering why your toe hurts. All along the path of your life you'll find brick walls. You can kick them, throw rocks at them, pound them with your fists, but it won't change the fact that the walls are there. You can say it isn't fair that the walls are there, and you can be very angry about it, but the walls won't move. You are stuck with the walls. You can choose to keep hurting your toe by kicking brick walls and expecting them to move for you, or you can accept the reality of walls across your path and look for effective ways to deal with them.

Allowing others' behavior to make you feel angry or upset is a choice. You can get hooked, or you can choose to work with your own inner creative force to change your responses so you don't take the hook. When others don't meet the caption on your expectation sign, you can consider their behavior as a wall in your path, and you can work on ideas for building a gate or finding a way over or around the wall. It gives you a chance to learn new methods of dealing with behavior and becoming effective in your relationships with others. The walls will be there whether you want them or not. Accept the reality and look at the situations as opportunities to learn more about gate-building.

When you allow others to make you feel bad, it is usually because you have your self-worth hooked into what they think of you. For Missie Meek to feel good about herself and her accomplishments, her mother had to approve of her. Missie could never do enough to get one hundred percent approval from her mother, so she felt inadequate. One expectation sign Missie carried was made from an old sign of her mother's. Its caption was, "In order for me to feel good, I have to meet the expectations on your sign so you'll feel good and approve of me for making you feel good." That's a pretty complicated sign, but Missie's mother gave out signals that clearly said, "For me to feel good, you have to be better than you are." Missie decided that before she could feel good about herself, her mother had to feel good. Unfortunately for Missie, she had a mother who would never be completely satisfied and give the approval that Missie so desperately thought she needed to feel good about herself. She went around with her sign that said, "What I need is for you to feel good about what

I do," and she was not able to get what she wanted or needed.

Taking Charge of Your Feelings

Before your toe will stop hurting, you have to stop kicking the wall. It is necessary for you to accept the unwanted reality of the wall across your path. Once you accept the reality, you can go for a change. If you are unable or unwilling to change what is outside of you, then you have no other choice than changing what is inside of you.

Changing Mr. Zero or Ms. Fauna was not within Greta Grumper's power. Getting angry didn't change them or the situations that bothered Greta. The possibility that Mr. Zero and Ms. Fauna would continue the same behavior was almost a hundred percent assured. Greta could go on resisting the unwanted reality and getting angry every time it happened (hurting her toe when she kicked the wall), or she could accept the fact that Ms. Fauna was inconsistent and Mr. Zero was a difficult person and decide what changes she could make so things would be easier for her. By her simple acceptance that Mr. Zero was not going to change and become an interesting lecturer who explains new concepts well, Greta could get rid of her expectation sign and stop being surprised and angry about his behavior.

If Art Affable accepts the reality of his parents' unfairness, he can begin to look for ways to deal with that unfairness. Accepting reality allows for options. When you get the focus off what you *can't* do, you can spend your energy on what you *can* do. In thinking about things that he could do, Art came up with this list.

1. Leave home.

2. "Have it out" with his parents.
3. Talk over the situation with his parents.
4. Get help from his school counselor on how to talk with his parents without anger.
5. Buy his own car.
6. Try to get one of his parents on his side.
7. Bribe his sister by offering to do her chores for a week if she'll let him use the car.
8. Develop a plan for sharing the car and submit it to his parents for consideration.
9. Use the money in his savings account to buy a one-way ticket to Siberia and put his sister on the airplane.
10. Find his sister a boyfriend so she won't need to use the car.
11. Find himself a girlfriend who has a car of her own.
12. Call the police and report his parents for child neglect.

Some of the items on Art's list were nutty fantasies that he threw in to satisfy some of his aggressive feelings and have a little fun, but there were some ideas that he could seriously follow up on and develop a realistic plan for getting around the wall of unfairness that was across his path. Once he accepted the reality of his parents' unfairness, he could begin to put his energies to work doing something constructive about the situation.

When you can't change something but maintain the need to change it, you are in a state of resistance. Resistance of reality caused Stephanie Stable a bad day. She was so upset by the way the little boy was treated by his mother that she felt miserable all day. The real cause of Stephanie's discomfort was her inability to do anything about what had happened. She had a real need to control that situation and make it different. The Voice in Stephanie's head kept "shoulding" on her. "Little children shouldn't be treated that way. Mothers should show love and understanding. You should be able to do something about that. You should have told her what you thought of her. You should have told the little boy that it wasn't his fault. You should have told her that he was just a little boy and it was an accident."

With the Voice "shoulding" all day, besides being angry Stephanie felt guilty because she didn't do anything. What was the reality of the situation? A mother treated her little boy disrespectfully and insensitively. Was Stephanie responsible for it in any way? No. Could she have done anything to change the situation? No. What was the only thing she could change? She could stop resisting reality and kicking the wall. All day long she was saying, "I hate this wall. It is insensitive, uncaring, and unfeeling. It shouldn't be this way. I don't like its being here at all. It makes me angry and upset every time I see it. I want it out of my path." She kept kicking and hurting.

Acceptance does not mean approval. By accepting the reality of the situation, Stephanie only admits that she can't do anything about it, that it is not in her power to change what happened or change that mother. Feeling angry or guilty won't do her any good. Once she stops resisting, she can do something constructive by looking at options. What are some of Stephanie's options in a situation that she can't control? She can:

1. Express her anger in an appropriate way so it doesn't build up inside of her.
2. Use it as a lesson in how not to treat her own children when she has children.
3. Plan a way to state her feelings appropriately to

the mother if a similar incident occurs in the
future.

4. Quit her job so she doesn't have to be around
people like that.
5. Tell her boss that people like that shouldn't be
allowed in the office.
6. Make it a point to be kind to the little boy the next
time he's in the office with his mother.
7. Accept that she can't do anything about what happened, acknowledge how sad it was for the little
boy, and feel her feelings of anger and sadness,
knowing that she doesn't have to do anything
about the feelings.
8. Stomp around and let everybody know that she's
angry and tell them why.
9. Mope around and feel bad all day.
10. Go after the woman and tell her what a terrible
mother she is.

Accepting reality opens up all kinds of options for expressing yourself. A variety of choices become possible,
even the choice to resist reality and feel bad. Missie Meek
thought that her only choice was to please her mother or
feel bad. Not until she faces the reality that her mother will
never be satisfied will Missie ever be able to satisfy herself.
To be good enough for herself, Missie has to stop trying to
be good enough for other people. She has to be able to say
to herself, "I worked hard and got a C on the test. That was
the best I could do on this test, and it's good enough. I am
an okay person who does the best work that I can." Missie
isn't an A student, and she can accept that reality even if
her mother won't.

After Missie accepts herself, she can make some decisions about how she will deal with the unrealistic expectations of her mother, but the most important task she has is to accept herself just the way she is. Because she accepts the unrealistic expectations of her mother and rejects who she is right now, Missie can't feel good about herself. No matter how hard she tries, she isn't going to be able to meet the unrealistic expectations she has placed on herself. When Missie accepts herself, instead of being frustrated about what she can't do, she will be able to make the choice to look at what she can do. Instead of feeling guilty and frustrated, she will feel good about what she does accomplish.

Acceptance

Accepting yourself is not an easy task because it requires that you suspend all value judgments. When you practice acceptance, you acknowledge all the facts about yourself but do not judge them as good or bad, right or wrong. It means not listening to the Voice's criticism as you look at who you are. Acceptance doesn't mean approval or disapproval. It simply means that you accept what is. For example, Missie might say, "I accept that I am a C student in most subjects and can get Bs in a few." That does not mean, "It's okay if I don't study because I can't get As anyway," or "I'm not smart because I don't get As." It means, "I accept that I have to work hard to get Bs and Cs and I don't always like that. Right now I'm not making any value judgments; I'm just accepting the facts."

In looking at some of her other behavior, Missie might say, "I accept that I don't stand up for myself," This doesn't mean that Missie likes or dislikes this about herself. She's not saying that not standing up for herself is something she approves of. She's not making a judgment of good or bad.

Learning to stand up for herself may be on her list of things she wants to work to improve, but right now that doesn't matter. All that matters is that she accept the fact that she doesn't stand up for herself.

Once you accept yourself, warts and all, you can go about the business of becoming the person you want to be. You can enjoy and build on your strengths and choose to work on your weaknesses one at a time. You can get rid of the negative labels that your Voice has hung on you. Throw out dumb, stupid, fat, bad student, wimp, screw-up, clumsy, klutz, bitchy, ugly, dull, bad personality, boring, shy, lazy, aggressive, skinny, flaky, pushy, and all the other negative things that the Voice might be calling you. Instead think of yourself in nonjudgmental terms. Bad student becomes, "I get Cs most of the time with an occasional D." Skinny becomes, "I weigh 105 pounds." Bitchy becomes, "On two occasions last week I was sarcastic to friends." Flaky becomes, "I locked my keys in the car twice in the last month." Ugly becomes, "I have a proportionately large nose, and right now my complexion is not perfect."

As important as getting rid of your negative labels is acknowledging your strengths. Stephanie Stable could make a list of strengths that would include, "I am sensitive to the feelings of others. I am responsible about getting to work on time. I do my chores at home with a minimum of grumbling on my part or reminding from my mother. My weight is in proportion to my height."

The list of strengths from Greta Grumper might include, "I do my homework on time. I listen to my friends. I have naturally curly hair that is easy to style."

You may find it difficult to accept your strengths because you don't feel comfortable. You may think you sound conceited. That's probably because you've had some experiences in your family that make it difficult for you to acknowledge your positive side. When you brought your report card home feeling so good about the five Bs you got, perhaps your father said. "How come you got a C?" Maybe you were excited about hitting the home run that won the game at recess, and your mother said, "I wish you could get half as excited about your spelling." Perhaps you were dressed for a date with someone special and knew you looked well, and your sister said, "Well, here comes Madame Queen. Don't you think you're wonderful!"

As a result of comments that put you down when you were up, you may feel very uncomfortable even thinking about your strengths. It may feel as if "somebody's gonna get you" if you say something good about yourself. That is the time to tell yourself that you're okay. Toot your horn, pat yourself on the back, acknowledge those positive things about yourself. You deserve the recognition! You've spent years listening to the Voice tell you negative, critical things. It's time to get even. Accepting yourself means accepting the positive about yourself.

Acceptance of Resistance

If you cannot accept a feeling, thought, or situation, accept your resistance to it. Don't fight the fact that you don't like to feel angry. Accept that you feel uncomfortable about being angry, that anger is not one of your favorite feelings. Your resistance builds when you try to fight how you are feeling. When you accept that you are resisting the feeling, it allows you to release the tension that would build with nonacceptance or resistance.

No matter what is happening in your life, you have the choice to accept or resist. If you choose to accept what is, you have the opportunity to explore options and move on

with your life. If you choose to resist reality, you'll stand
and kick walls and never move. What you do about the
walls in your path is up to you. It has nothing to do with
like or enjoy or approve. It has to do with acceptance of
reality and feeling good about yourself as a capable, competent, self-respecting human being.

CHAPTER 5

The Inner Voice That
Attacks Self-esteem

T he first day of answering the phone and making appointments at Harriet's Beauty Salon was finally over for Kay Kind. She was sure that even though her employer was her mother's best friend whom she called Aunt Harri, she would be fired after only one day. Kay had made every mistake possible to make. Even though Aunt Harri had assured her that her mistakes were the kind that everybody made when they first started, Kay was sure that Aunt Harri was just being polite. Over and over the Voice in Kay's head said, "You are so dumb. You can't even work a simple phone system with four lines. Any ten-year-old could learn the difference between the hold button and the intercom button. You didn't just cut one person off today, you did it twice. Why can't you ever do anything right? Aunt Harri acted like it was no big deal when you found out you had booked two appointments for her day off, but she was probably disgusted. Then you forgot to get their phone numbers so you could call them back and change the appointments. She told you to get phone numbers for everybody who called. How could you forget something so important? You really are stupid, to say nothing of being incompetent. Those two women are going to be furious when they come in and have to have a different hairdresser because you messed up. If you haven't been fired already, they'll probably tell Aunt Harri to fire you then and there. You'd better try harder to-morrow so you don't embarrass yourself more in front of everybody."

As she walked home, Kay was sure that everyone on the street could look at her and know that she had been a dis-aster at the shop. When she walked in the door and her mother asked how her first day on the job was, she burst into tears. She didn't know if she could go back the next day.

After three weeks working at Pizza Place, Larry Leery knew most of the regulars. He worked from 4 to 8 four evenings a week. One really cute girl named Karen came in almost every day for a super size Pepsi. She seemed to like Larry and always hung around to talk if it wasn't busy. After Karen left, Larry always wished he had asked for her phone number, but while she was there he couldn't get up the courage to ask. The Voice in his head always said, "What makes you think she could like you anyway? She's much too cute to bother with you. She could get someone a lot better looking than you. She's just a friendly person and would be the same no matter who was here. Besides, if you had her number, you'd probably bore her to death if you said anything at all. You know you always freeze on the phone, and then she'd think you were stupid. What if you asked for her phone number and she didn't give it to you?

That would be awful. She probably only talks to you because she feels sorry for you. She can tell that you have trouble talking to girls so she's doing you a favor by talking to you."

After Karen would leave, the Voice would say, "Well, you missed your chance again. You should have at least got her phone number even if you didn't ask her out. You really are a loser."

Looking as though she hadn't a care in the world, Wendy Wonderful walked out of the school building toward the parking lot. If she could get to her car and leave without anyone stopping her, she would be all right. This had been the worst day she'd had in a long time, and she just wanted to be alone. The Voice in her head had been going since first period when she got back her history report with a B- on it. She had needed an A in order to get an A on her report card. All day all Wendy heard was, "You are in for it now. You knew you needed an A, and you waited until the last minute to do the assignment. No wonder you got such a low grade. You should have started sooner. You should have known that it would take longer than usual to do the report because you had to go to the library. There was no excuse for getting a B-. You just didn't try hard enough. Mom and Dad are going to be so disappointed. You really let them down."

At lunch Wendy had saved a place for Kay Kind, but she had forgotten to save one for Polly Perfect. Wendy could see how disappointed Polly was that she couldn't sit at their table. Her Voice really got her on that one too. "How do you expect to keep friends when you treat them like that? You know there are always six of you who sit together. You should have counted chairs more carefully. You know how it feels to be left out, and now you did that to Polly. Even though you did apologize, it doesn't change the fact that you hurt her feelings. You should call her tonight and ask her to meet you before lunch tomorrow so you'll be able to sit together for sure. Don't be surprised if she doesn't want to talk to you. She probably thinks you're getting stuck up since you can drive the car to school."

The final episode in Wendy's glorious day happened during P.E. She hated it when they played softball because she couldn't catch fly balls. All the time she was dressing her Voice was saying, "What if they put you outfield and you're near where the boys are playing? That would be awful. If a fly ball comes and bounces off your head or your chest, everybody will laugh. That would be awful. You'll look so stupid."

Sure enough, Wendy was put in the outfield on the side nearest the boys, and of course, four fly balls came her way. Two went over her head as she ran forward, one bounced right in front of her after she backed away, and the fourth one hit her glove and went by her. The Voice didn't let up on her the whole period. "You should have stayed right where you were and you might have caught that one. You looked so stupid the guys probably won't stop laughing for days...Not another one! You take the prize for letting your team down. They must all hate you for keeping them out here like this, to say nothing of the fun the boys will have telling about your marvelous catching ability...Oh, watch out, here comes another one. It looks like it's going to hit you. Why did you back up? You could have caught that one! One more time you keep your team outfield...You should at least try to catch the ball. You always try to get away from it. The team is never going to get off the field with you out here. All somebody needs to do is get it in the air and you're in a panic. Oh, look out, here comes another one. At least get close to it this time. Oh, no, right off the end of your glove. You're such a klutz. . ."

Whenever the team was infield, Wendy sat as far as she could from her team captain, Alice Athleet. She could tell that Alice was really disgusted with her. Near the end of the period, Wendy's team was up and only needed one run to tie the score. While Wendy waited for her turn at bat, the Voice was still talking to her, "What if you get up and can't even hit the ball? That would be awful. Suppose you strike out? Then everybody will be mad at you. This has not been your day. With everything else that's happened, you probably won't get a hit." It had definitely not been Wendy's day, and of course she didn't get a hit; and now all she wanted to do was get to the car and be by herself.

The Critical Voice in Your Head

Studying the environment has been part of your education since early elementary school. As a nation we're so concerned about the environment that the government has an Environmental Protection Agency. Even though the outer environment is very important, you have a far more important inner environment of which you may be completely unaware. That inner environment, your emotional world, is influenced by a constant dialog that affects your feelings, behavior, and self-esteem. That inner Voice may be underground operating automatically and unnoticed. If it isn't brought to your attention, it does its destructive work and you never know why you are feeling so upset.

Another part of your inner environment is your Inner Being, who is your best friend. Your Inner Being is where your true feelings are. It's the beautiful, positive, supportive part of you. Unfortunately, the feelings of your Inner

Being are often forced out or blocked by the critical Voice that pushes, prods, nags, criticizes, and punishes you. The Voice works against the positive life force of your Inner Being.

Origins of the Voice

All your life people have talked to you. They sent you messages with words, looks, and actions. Your subconscious mind took in all those messages. At first your parents and your family gave you all your messages, but as you've grown, more and more people outside your family have influenced you—friends, teachers, friends' parents, neighbors, girlfriends, boyfriends, classmates, everyone with whom you've had contact. All along the way your Voice has picked up messages that were negative or that you interpreted in negative ways, and it used them to limit your self-expression and mental and emotional growth.

You built your self-image, how you see yourself, on what other people told you about you. If someone made comments about your big feet when you were ten years old, barely five feet tall, and wore a size ten shoe, your Voice may still tell you that you have big feet at seventeen when you're 6'2", weigh 190 pounds, and wear a size 11 shoe. Compared to the rest of you, your feet aren't big, but the Voice doesn't change its negative message. Often people who are treated in unloving ways by family or by people whose approval they want will subconsciously draw an incorrect conclusion about themselves. They will decide that they are unlovable rather than accepting the truth that the family members are unloving. As a result, the message the Voice sends whenever they are treated disrespectfully or in an uncaring way is, "You don't deserve to be well treated. You're unworthy. You're just no good." Even if others tell them that they deserve to be treated better, the Voice never changes its message.

Besides not changing its message, the Voice doesn't allow new positive messages in, but it grabs negative ones right away. To test yourself on that, think of all the positive comments you've received in the past week. Now think of all the critical comments you've received. Which were easier to recall? Did the thought of the criticisms bring up uncomfortable feelings? Did you notice that your Voice put in some extra negative comments of its own? The Voice blames you when things go wrong, calls you names like "stupid" or "klutz" when you make a mistake, or tells you what everyone else is thinking—which always happens to be negative toward you. Perfection is the dominant expectation of the Voice. In any situation there is a clear right way. When you don't perform absolutely perfectly, the Voice becomes preoccupied with what was wrong, and it tells you over and over how you messed up. In short, the Voice tears down your self-esteem and keeps you from feeling good about yourself.

The Voice Keeps You from Your Inner Being

Your emotions give you information that you can't get through logic and thinking. There are times when you just know that something is the right thing to do. You just "have a feeling" about it. There are other times when your emotions send you a strong "No." Then it's time to back off, because if you go against your feelings you'll end up saying, "I knew I shouldn't have done that. I should have followed my feelings."

Some people seem to be very lucky, and when you ask them, they say, "I had a hunch..." Hunches and feelings are your emotions giving you information that you can't get from your mind. The Voice keeps you away from your Inner Being by discounting your feelings. It will say to you, "Big deal, you have a feeling that riding home with Dan Dawdle isn't a good idea. He's leaving right now and Dave Dependable won't be leaving for a half hour. You'll get home sooner if you ride with Dan." All the while your feelings tell you that Dan never goes straight home even though he's promised to drive you straight home. The Voice says, "He said he wasn't stopping anywhere, so he'll take you right home." The middle of your gut is telling you that Dan doesn't do what he says he'll do, but the Voice wins after a few more things like, "Don't be silly; don't act so superior, you're being stupid; it's a half hour head start, you should be grateful he's willing to go two miles out of his way," and you end up a half hour late getting home.

That process of discounting your feelings is a denial of your Inner Being. When someone says something that hurts your feelings and you stuff it inside when the Voice says, "You shouldn't be so thin-skinned," you are denying your Inner Being. When your natural reaction to an injustice is to be angry and the Voice says, "Don't make a big deal out of nothing," and you pretend you didn't notice, you are denying your Inner Being. When you feel sad and want to cry and the Voice says, "Don't act like a baby," and you don't cry, you are denying your Inner Being. When you win the prize and want to jump and shout and the Voice says, "Don't act stupid," and you act "cool" instead, you are denying your Inner Being. After you do that for a while, you lose touch with your true feelings and you no longer trust your feelings.

With the separation from your feelings comes a separation from your Inner Being. You become detached from that beautiful part of yourself and can't know it because of the negative input from the Voice that makes you feel unworthy and no good. You get a steady message of, "You're not good enough." Not good enough always sends you on an "approval search." You do all kinds of things for approval from others, but nothing is ever good enough. No matter what Aunt Harri said, Kay's Voice wouldn't have accepted that Kay was doing all right. Even if everyone on the team played worse than Wendy did and told her she was fun to have on the team, the Voice would have told her she wasn't good enough. With the Voice judging you, your self-worth is on the line every minute. No matter how much approval you get from outside, the Voice will not accept it. You will never feel good for very long if you seek approval from outside because the Voice won't allow you to believe it. Feeling good about yourself is an inside job, and in order to allow your Inner Being to flourish, to grow and bloom and thrive, you have to control the Voice.

Reprogramming the Voice

Your subconscious mind will believe anything you tell it, and it will help you live what you say you are. However, if you aren't aware of the Voice, it will be the one that the subconscious listens to. Lots of people put on a big front of how wonderful they are. Remember Brad Brasher, who wanted everyone to think he was hip, slick, and cool, but underneath his big talk his Voice was telling him that he was nothing. Brad had to act big because he felt so small inside. Wendy Wonderful spent her day trying to look as though she were having a great day while her Voice scolded and punished her all day. It's not what *you* say to cover your fears and your feelings, it's what the *Voice* says that counts.

To do anything about the Voice, you have to be aware of

what your Voice is saying to you. Whenever something happens, it is not the event but what you tell yourself about it that determines its importance. When Greg Garious bumped into Barry Belligerent in the hall, Barry's Voice said, "Who does he think he is bumping into you like that?" and Barry got angry. When Mark Merit bumped into Patrick Pushover in the hall, Patrick's Voice said, "Mark sure bumped into you hard. What did you do to make him mad at you?" and Patrick felt guilty. When Harry Hardy bumped into Mark Merit, Mark's Inner Being said, "Harry must have been watching where he's been instead of where he's going," and Mark felt fine because he had a supportive Inner Being that was not ruled by his Voice, so he gave Harry the benefit of the doubt. There were three very different responses to the same event because of the differences in what the Voice told each person.

It's important to become aware of your Voice because you can't change the dialog until you know what the Voice is saying. Then you can work on developing a supportive inner environment. You can appreciate and like yourself. The Voice will tell you that liking yourself is being conceited, but that's a lie just like everything else the Voice says. Conceit is an exaggerated estimate of yourself. Self-support is appreciating the truth about yourself and assessing it accurately.

MESSAGES FROM THE VOICE

Since the Voice is very sneaky and you may not have known about it before, you need to listen carefully to what it is saying to you. You need to know the typical messages that the Voice uses so you can begin to deal effectively with it. Remember that no matter what the message is, *the*

Voice always lies. Some of the things the Voice says seem to be true, but there is always a flaw because the Voice always lies.

Negative Labels

Labeling you dumb, stupid, klutz, or loser is a favorite with the Voice. Most people are so used to that kind of thing that they don't realize it's one of the sneaky tricks of the Voice. Because she couldn't work a telephone with four lines perfectly the first day she used it, Kay's Voice called her dumb. When Larry Leery didn't get Karen's phone number, his Voice called him a loser. Before she even got on the playing field, Wendy's Voice told her that she was going to "look so stupid." It's pretty hard to feel good about yourself with those kinds of labels put on you.

Your tricky, sneaky Voice uses labels in other ways too. Whenever you want to do something that is a little risky, the Voice stops you with negative labels. Larry Leery wanted Karen's phone number, but the Voice told him that he would be "boring" and then she'd think he was "stupid," so Larry was stopped in his tracks.

Another trick of the Voice is to use what seems like a good label to stop you. Maybe you're really tired and want to go home and crash on the couch and watch TV when a friend asks you to help her with her math homework. You usually don't mind helping, but today you really want to go home. The Voice says, "If you were a good friend you'd help her." So, being a good friend, you don't do what you really want to do and you help your friend instead. Helping friends is a good thing to do, but stuffing your own feelings usually makes you feel obligated and resentful toward your friend for asking you.

The Voice has other ways of using labels against you.

Wendy had a "low" grade on her report. Because it wasn't an A, the Voice told her it was low. There are plenty of people who would be delighted to have a B- and would call it a high grade. Larry didn't get a phone number so his Voice told him he was a loser. Since he wasn't a winner at everything, he was a loser. That kind of labeling is called global labeling because it takes one small behavior or incident and labels you universally. Global labels most often have to do with your appearance, performance, or intelligence. When Wendy Wonderful gained a pound, the Voice said, "You're going to be a fat slob if you keep this up." Larry Leery didn't like to call girls on the phone because the Voice said, "You'll probably bore her to death." Patrick Pushover's Voice said, "You're such a wimp," because he didn't want to fight Kevin Kombat. Harry Hardy looked at the braces on his teeth and his Voice said, "You're ugly." Nothing else is taken into account. The Voice sees one small deviation from perfect and gives the whole thing a negative label.

Some of the phrases that let you know the Voice is using negative labels are: "Don't be bitchy." "Don't be selfish." "Don't be unkind." "Don't be so grouchy." "Don't be mean." "You sound conceited." "You're too sensitive." "You're so stupid." "You're such a klutz." "They'll think you're stuck up." "You're a failure." "You're a quitter." "You're so clumsy." "You're so dumb." "You're hopeless." "You're worthless." "You're awful." "You're a rotten player."

The labels the Voice gives you are all lies. They range from flat-out untrue to gross exaggeration. Become aware of the labels so you can intercept the message. In the next chapter you will learn ways to give yourself support against the attacks of the Voice once you know how it is bombarding you.

Filtering

The Voice is very selective about the messages it keeps on file to use. When anything positive comes your way, the Voice filters it out, discounts it, tells you that you don't deserve it, but when anything negative or critical is said to you or about you the Voice stores it away to use later. The filtering process is very sneaky. Aunt Harri told Kay not to worry about her mistakes, but the Voice told her that Aunt Harri was just being polite. Karen enjoyed talking to Larry Leery, but his Voice filtered that out and told Larry that she only talked to him because she felt sorry for him. Wendy's entire day was a case of filtering by the Voice. According to the Voice, nothing good happened that day. There had to have been some bright spots, but Wendy couldn't see them for the clouds of negativity that the Voice brought.

Certain clues will let you know when filtering is going on. If you feel uncomfortable when people give you compliments, you are probably filtering. Responses like, "This old thing?" "It was really nothing." are indicators that the Voice is discounting the compliment. When the Voice keeps telling you how terrible something is, how long it's going to take, how much it hurts, how put-down you feel, you can bet that it is filtering out all the positive things that would help you deal with the situation.

Think about what happened and see what you remember. If you can only remember the negative events, you're like Wendy, who could only think of the four flies she missed and forgot about the ground ball that she threw to second to start the double play. She brushed aside the long throw from the outfield that got the runner out at third instead of being a triple. She was so embarrassed by the strike out that she discounted the home run she hit that tied the game in the first place. With the filter well in place, the Voice did a number on Wendy that made for a miserable day. Yours does the same for you.

Overgeneralization

To arrive at a generalization you observe the data, develop a theory, test the theory, and then make your generalization. To overgeneralize, you take one piece of data and draw your conclusion without investigating or testing out your idea. The Voice is great at overgeneralizing. "You can't even work a simple phone system with four lines. Any ten-year-old could learn the difference between the hold button and the intercom button." Kay made two mistakes the first day she used a four-button phone, and her Voice told her she was less intelligent than a ten-year-old. The Voice took something small and generalized it to all-around stupidity.

Kay's Voice was so successful at making her feel bad with overgeneralizations that it used them often. "Why can't you ever do anything right?" doesn't give Kay credit for what she does do right—which is almost everything. "You'd better try harder so you don't embarrass yourself more in front of everybody." Who's everybody? Very few people were involved with Kay's mistakes at the shop, but the Voice generalized to everybody. Larry's Voice did its number with overgeneralizations too. "You know you always freeze on the phone." "Always" means there's never a time when Larry talks freely; however, he has no problem talking to his friends.

"You take the prize for letting your team down," was one of the Voice's overgeneralizations for Wendy. She'd made some important contributions to the game, but a missed fly blew away all the good, according to the Voice. "The team is never going to get off the field with you out here," was another goodie from Wendy's Voice. "Never" is a good clue to overgeneralizations. Some other words that let you know the Voice is overgeneralizing are *always, all, everybody, nobody, any, every, none, everything, everyone, nothing.*

Mind Reading

Deciding what people are thinking and feeling and what they will say is a way the Voice keeps you anxious, worried, upset, and feeling bad about yourself. Kay was afraid of losing her job because the Voice read the minds of the customers. "Those two women are going to be furious when they come in...they'll probably tell Aunt Harri to fire you then and there." The Voice told Kay that she was dumb and incompetent, so naturally she believed the Voice when it told her that everyone else thought she was dumb and incompetent too. Mind reading is destructive to self-esteem because the critical Voice tells you that others are judging you just as critically and negatively as it does.

Larry's Voice did a good job of mind reading and making him feel bad about himself. "She probably only talks to you because she feels sorry for you. She can tell that you have trouble talking to girls [She reads minds too.] so she's doing you a favor by talking to you."

When Polly didn't have a place to sit at the table, Wendy apologized, but her Voice said, "Don't be surprised if she won't talk to you. She probably thinks you're getting stuck up..." The Voice told Wendy what the others were thinking about her softball playing. "They must all hate you for keeping them out here...to say nothing of the fun the boys will have telling about your marvelous catching ability." "...everybody will be mad at you." Because the critical Voice had judged her so harshly, Wendy believed that others judged her the same way.

Mind reading will cause you to avoid people. Wendy decided to sit as far from Alice as possible because the Voice told her that Alice was disgusted with her. After school Wendy just wanted to get to her car and be by herself. She couldn't face people because she felt so bad. Kay didn't know if she could go back to work because the Voice told her over and over that others thought she was incompetent.

Mind reading is not only unfair to you, it is unfair to the people about whom you've made assumptions. The Voice doesn't have to work hard to get you to believe that it knows what people are thinking, feeling, or going to say. The Voice always seems so positive that you go right along with it. You don't check with the people whose minds are being read to see if the "reading" is correct. The Voice tells you it isn't necessary to check it out because, of course, it *knows*. As a result of believing the mind reading of the Voice, you cause yourself and others unnecessary pain and alienation.

Awfulizing

The Voice likes to play "What if. . . ? That would be awful." "What if you asked for her phone number and she didn't give it to you? That would be awful." "What if they put you outfield and you're near where the boys are playing? That would be awful." "If a fly ball comes and bounces off your head or your chest, everybody will laugh. That would be awful." "What if you get up and can't hit the ball? That would be awful." That kind of "awfulizing" keeps you stuck and feeling anxious.

When the Voice "What ifs" you, it is really saying, "I

happen to know beyond the shadow of a doubt that this awful thing is going to happen. You'd just as well give up right now and accept that your future is going to look like this." What's so awful about it anyway? If Karen doesn't give Larry her phone number when he asks, he'll feel stupid and embarrassed. If the boys laugh at Wendy, she'll feel embarrassed. If she doesn't hit the ball, she'll feel embarrassed. Most of the "What ifs" have feelings of embarrassment or hurt pride as the "awful" that will happen. Most of the "What ifs" don't happen, and if the "awful" embarrassment comes, you'll survive. The worst part of the "awfulizing" is the feeling of anxiety that something terrible is going to happen. The Voice wants you to believe that you will die if the "awful" happens, but you don't. You even have the choice to feel bad or good about what happens. The choice is always yours.

Be Perfect

For most people, in one way or another, the Voice is saying, "Be perfect." Kay felt so terrible because she was not doing her job perfectly. She was dumb, incompetent, unforgivable, people would be furious with her—all the things the Voice was saying added up to "YOU ARE NOT PERFECT." Wendy's "Be perfect" button was really pushed all day long. The punishment being handed out had a lot to do with not being perfect. She didn't get a perfect grade. She made a mistake by not saving Polly a seat since her Voice let her know that she was the only one in the group responsible for doing that sort of thing. She was not a perfect softball player. All day long her imperfection brought the criticism of the Voice.

Many times when the Voice is handing out negative labels it is really saying, "You're not perfect. You're not good enough." Larry's Voice didn't say, "You're ugly." It said, "She could get someone a lot better looking than you," which translates to, "You're not good-looking enough. You're not perfect." Kay's Voice said, "You're so dumb." She was "so dumb" because she didn't handle the telephones perfectly; she wasn't good enough. Wendy was "klutz" because she didn't catch the ball; she didn't do it right; she wasn't good enough. So underneath many of the Voice's messages is another one that says, "You have to be perfect or you're no good."

With the Voice there is no middle ground. You are either wonderful or awful, right or wrong, good or bad. You get the A or you feel like a failure. You look like a 10 or you're a 1. In anything you do you're a 1 or a 10, according to the Voice; 2 through 9 don't count.

Guilt Trips

To keep you feeling guilty and bad about yourself, the Voice "shoulds" on you. "You *should* have at least got her phone number..." made Larry feel as though he had done something bad. "You *should* have started sooner," made Wendy feel guilty that she waited to do her paper. "You *should* have known it would take longer than usual..." "You *should* have counted chairs more carefully...You *should* call her tonight...You *should* have stayed right where you were...You *should* at least try to catch the ball." Wendy's Voice just "should" all over her all day, and she felt guilty because she didn't do all the things the Voice told her she "should" do.

The Voice uses "shouldn't" just as effectively. "You *shouldn't* say you hate your brother." "You *shouldn't* hang up on people even if they are rude." "You *shouldn't* leave your room in such a mess." "You *shouldn't* be late to class."

"You *shouldn't* be mad at your mother." Some of the things that the Voice "shoulds" and "shouldn'ts" on you about are positive. It's a good idea to get to class on time. It's good to be kind and thoughtful to others.

The problem with "shoulds" comes as a result of your internal response to the Voice. As soon as you hear "should," it becomes "have to," and "shouldn't" is the same as "must not." You feel obligated to obey the "should" of the Voice. Suppose you're sitting watching TV and you remember that you promised to call a friend. You want to talk to this friend, and your Voice says, "You should call Friend." Immediately you feel as though you have to call your friend. If you don't call your friend, you'll feel guilty. Suppose you've been talking to your counselor, have just enough time to get to class, but need to stop at your locker to get your book. You have a good reason for being late to class, but your Voice says, "You shouldn't be late for class, Mr. Zero's not going to like it." The message you get is, "You must not be late for class," and you feel guilty when you are.

Other words from the Voice that set up the guilt trip are "could" and "ought." "How *could* you forget...," said Kay's Voice, and she felt guilty. Wendy's ever critical Voice gave her the guilt when it said, "You *could* have caught that one." When your Voice says, "You *ought* to know better," the guilt piles on. "Must" and "have to" are also used by the Voice, as in, "You *must* get up early tomorrow to study some more for the test," or "You *have to* get these books back to the library." Since it's midnight and you set the alarm for 5 a.m., is it any wonder you don't want to get up to study? But you feel guilty if you don't. When the books don't get back to the library but sit on the chair for a week, every day you look at them and feel guilty while the Voice reminds you that you have to get them back to the library.

Sometimes you do hurt people and feel bad about it. At those times it is appropriate to feel remorse. You regret what happened and are truly distressed because of your behavior, so you take action to correct the wrong. Then you can stop punishing yourself. However, if the punishment continues the Voice has taken over with its guilt-producing "should," "could," "ought," "must," or "have to."

Although "could," "ought," "must," and "have to" are very effective in making you punish yourself and feel guilty, "should" is the Voice's favorite guilt-maker. When you sense that you are into punishing yourself because the guilt feelings are persisting, look for the "shoulds." In one way or another the Voice is "shoulding" on you when those feelings hang on, and you end up sitting in a pile of "should."

You're Not Okay

Underlying most of the negative messages that the Voice sends is a strong message that you are not okay, that you are not a good person. It makes you feel undeserving, no good, and worthless. Kay Kind was trying so hard to be perfect and do the best possible job, but her expectation was too high to meet. She did the best she possibly could, but the Voice said it wasn't good enough. Kay believed the Voice and felt so bad because she wasn't perfect that she ended up crying. She felt she had been a disaster at the shop. Notice that she felt *she* had been the disaster. Her day wasn't a disaster. Kay was the disaster. Her Voice was sneaky and didn't say it loudly, but the message was, "You weren't perfect so you're no good. Your worth depends on your behavior and performance, and you failed today. You are worthless."

Larry Leery could hardly get his mouth open to talk to Karen because the Voice was so actively negative whenever she was around. "What makes you thinks she could like you anyway? She's much too cute to bother with you." The unspoken message from the Voice was "You're not good enough for Karen." If it were any other girl the message would be the same. The only other message the Voice might give would be the one from the joke: "You wouldn't want to be seen with anyone who would stoop low enough to go out with you." It's as though Larry's Voice has been saying, "Something's wrong with you. You're not an okay person."

Larry wasn't perfect. In some things he didn't mind not being perfect. He got Bs and Cs in school and was satisfied with that, but in relationships with people, especially girls, he felt like a total nothing. His Voice told him that he didn't know how to talk to people, and it was his fault. There was something wrong with him because other people didn't have any trouble talking to each other. The Voice told Larry he wasn't very good-looking either, because of his hair and freckles. Carrot red hair was not okay, and he had freckles—not little ones; big, huge freckles. According to the Voice's standard of perfection, Larry didn't measure up, and he felt "less than," "not enough."

When the Voice filters out all the positive things that people say to you, it leaves you with the message that you're not okay. By discounting the good—"You didn't do anything special," "If they knew how you are at home they wouldn't say that," "Anybody could have done that"—the Voice leaves you with only the bad stuff that says, "You're not an okay person. There's something wrong with you." Mind reading, awfulizing, overgeneralizing, and labeling all send the same message. How can you possibly feel good about yourself when your Inner Being is attacked constantly by your critical Voice, when you are continually bombarded with messages that you are not okay?

Changing the Voice Messages

Dealing with the Voice takes skill and practice. Changing that inner dialog can be done. It begins with becoming aware of what the Voice is saying to you. For at least a week, each day write down the negative messages that the Voice gives you. After you have written down what the Voice is saying to you, go over your list and decide what specific message the Voice is sending. A good way to do this is to fold a paper in half lengthwise and put what the Voice says on one side of the paper and what the message is on the other. Your paper might look like this:

Voice Statements	Message
You're so dumb.	Negative Label
You always mess up.	Overgeneralization
They'll think you're stupid if you do that.	Mind Reading
You shouldn't feel that way.	Guilt Trip
Can't you do anything right?	Overgeneralization
	Guilt Trip
	Be Perfect
	You're Not Okay
She really didn't mean that, she's just being nice.	Filtering
You didn't study hard enough.	You're Not Okay
	Be Perfect
He'll never forgive you.	Guilt Trip
	Mind Reading
	You're Not Okay
What if you trip and fall when you get up to give your report? That would be awful.	Awfulizing

After you've written down the Voice messages and labeled them, you'll be more aware of how the Voice is controlling you. You'll probably find a few that are special favorites of your Voice. As time goes on you'll be able to do the Voice analysis in your head, but to begin with you must write it down.

Once you know what the Voice is saying to you, you'll be ready to fight it and replace it with positive inner dialog. That positive inner dialog comes from your Inner Being, and it requires getting tuned in to your Inner Being and developing a supportive, protective atmosphere for its growth. Your Inner Being can grow only when your true feelings are acknowledged, accepted, and valued. That's done in two ways—by talking back to the Voice and by being assertive in protecting the rights of your Inner Being.

CHAPTER 6

Talking Back to the Voice

As the group settled into the circle of chairs that Frank Friendly, the church youth minister, had set out earlier, some of the young people took out notebooks, others took out sheets of paper, and a few looked guilty. Frank smiled at the ones who looked guilty and asked, "What is the Voice saying to you right now?" Larry Leery grinned and said, "You did it again. How could you forget to bring your notebook?" Then Felicia Fetching chimed in with, "Everybody's going to think you're stupid." "You should have put it out where you could see it on your way out the door," was Stephanie Stable's offering. Even those who had their notes began to join in, and soon the entire group was laughing.

Frank was glad to have such an enthusiastic response from the group. It showed that they were getting in touch with the critical Voice and were interested in doing something about it. The week before, they had discussed eight common Voice messages and had decided to write down and label the messages they heard from the Voice during the week. That was the reason for the notebooks and papers. This week they were going to share, and then Frank was going to give them some ways to talk back to the Voice.

As she stood in the doorway of her counseling office, Ms. Mentor saw Kay Kind and noticed that Kay wasn't her usual sparkly self. After exchanging greetings with Kay, Ms. Mentor asked her if she wanted to talk. A little hesitant at first, Kay was soon telling Ms. Mentor about how terrible her first day of work had been and how she wasn't sure she wanted to go to work today. Ms. Mentor's first comment to Kay was, "What are you telling yourself?" That began the first of several talks Kay had with Ms. Mentor about the messages of the Voice and how to talk back to it.

Telling her mother about the little boy who knocked over the plant and was mistreated by his mother, Stephanie Stable gut angry again. Her mother, Stella, listened and then said, "Steph, you're 'shoulding' all over that lady and yourself too." When she saw the questioning look on her daughter's face, Stella began to share with Stephanie some of the things she had learned in a cognitive training class she had taken a few weeks before. Stella told her daughter that getting in touch with the inner dialog and the critical Voice was the first step to creating a supportive inner environment. She shared her workshop notes and some of the books she'd been reading with Stephanie. Learning to talk back to the Voice was a long-term project that they could work on together.

• • •

When he read the book *Coping Through Assertiveness* by Rhoda McFarland, Mark Merit got in touch with the Voice in his head. He knew that the Voice was making his life miserable, so he began to search for other books that would give him more information about how to deal with it. He learned that the term psychologists use for changing the way you think is cognitive-behavior therapy. That led him to several books that gave him ways to talk back to the Voice.

Learning to Talk Back to the Voice

Talking back to the Voice may seem strange to you at first. Working with a group or with another person makes it easier. In groups you benefit from the sharing of others and the knowledge that others are experiencing the same thing you are. Forgetting his notes became no big deal when Larry Leery realized that everyone in the group understood how he felt and knew what was going on in his head. It became a joke, and the Voice lost that round with the whole group.

If you don't know of a group that's working on talking back to the Voice, perhaps you can find a counselor, teacher, minister, parent, relative, or friend to work with you. Kay Kind was fortunate that Ms. Mentor saw her and understood how punishing her Voice was. Because she knew the ways of the Voice, Ms. Mentor didn't try to cheer Kay up and make her feel better. She began working with Kay on taking some of the power away from the Voice.

Stephanie Stable was lucky because her mother was "into" assertiveness and self-actualizing. She had someone who could not only help her but also model the behavior for her. They were able to practice their Voice-fighting techniques together.

Sharing with someone else makes it easier, but if you have no one to share with, you can learn to talk back to your Voice and support your Inner Being on your own the way Mark did. It takes longer, and the lack of feedback and sharing can make it tougher. The Voice tries to get in and give you feedback on how you're handling it! (Of course, you'll be handling it all wrong.) The Voice doesn't give up.

Rules for Talking Back to the Voice

1. Remember that THE VOICE ALWAYS LIES.
2. Be very firm with the Voice. Whenever you can, talk out loud to the Voice. When you can't talk out loud, shout in your head. Tell the Voice to *Shut up* or *Buzz off*. (Swear at it if you feel like it!)
3. NEVER agree with the Voice.
4. Remember that the Voice is FAST and SNEAKY.
5. Write down your Back Talk to the Voice ahead of time so you won't have to worry about thinking it up when you need it.

To talk back to the Voice, you must know what it's saying. If you haven't written down your Voice messages and analyzed them yet, you can't talk back. You can't fight what you don't know. When you're sick and go to the doctor, she doesn't write a prescription and then examine you.

When you've completed the analysis of your Voice messages and have labeled them all, you're ready to organize your campaign for talking back effectively. Get eight pieces of paper or 5 × 8 cards and label each one with a message category. On the left side of the paper or card write down messages from your Voice. One of your cards might look like this.

BE PERFECT

- You really messed up this time.
- You were lucky to get credit for that.
- Look how wrinkled your shirt is.
- Do that over, you made a mistake.
- You could have done better.
- You're so careless.
- You'd better do more so you'll be best.
- You hurt her feelings.

When you have a card or paper for each category, you're ready to choose your Back Talk for the Voice. Examples of appropriate Back Talk for each category are given below. Choose the ones that fit what your Voice says to you. Better yet, use the examples to help you write your own Back Talk. Then write your Back Talk beside the Voice messages in each category so you'll be able to refer to it whenever you need it.

Negative Labels

Negative labels are not true or accurate evaluations of you, and you don't have to accept them. The Voice wants you to believe them and repeat them, but you can choose to reject them and substitute more supportive, positive statements about yourself.

BACK TALK FOR NEGATIVE LABELS

- I'm not stupid; I'm inexperienced.
- I'm not dumb; I'm learning a new skill.
- I'm not conceited; I do play tennis very well.
- I'm not stuck up; I'm sometimes too shy to speak.
- I'm not a klutz; I'm a beginner.

- I'm not bitchy; it's okay to express my anger.
- I'm not being selfish; I'm taking care of myself.
- I'm not a quitter; I have done the best I can.
- I'm not being stubborn; I'm standing up for myself.
- I refuse to call myself names anymore.
- Stop calling me ugly! I'm a beautiful person.
- Shut up! I'm not a loser because of one mistake.
- Buzz off! I don't want to listen to that.
- Get off my back, Voice!
- Get lost!

Choose your Back Talk from this list or make your own, but write at least one statement of support beside each of the negative labels your Voice is putting on you. It's a good idea to have two or three ways to back-talk the Voice, because it will not be quiet with just one statement from you. Wendy Wonderful's Voice called her a klutz because she had difficulty catching fly balls. When Wendy used Back Talk, the conversation went like this:

Voice Message	Back Talk
You're such a klutz.	I have difficulty catching fly balls. I'm not a klutz.
You sure look like a klutz.	Not catching flies doesn't make me a klutz.
You're just uncoordinated.	I'm a good dancer and I'm a good basketball player. Don't give me that uncoordinated stuff.
You look like a klutz in the outfield.	Buzz off, Voice! I don't want to listen to you any more.
You...	Just shut up!

Since you know how your Voice "picks on" you, you can practice ahead of time. You can be ready for the next attack. If the Voice gets you before you practice, go over that battle and work out how you would fight it more effectively; then have your Back Talk ready for the next time.

Filtering

You will know you're filtering when you only hear the negative things the Voice is saying to you and disregard the positive comments from others. When your whole day is all bad, your Voice has put the filter up. If you ignore the positive comments but remember the one negative, the Voice has been filtering.

BACK TALK FOR FILTERING

- My backhand was off today, but my serve was good.
- There you go making something big out of nothing.
- You're just trying to make me feel bad. I did a good job.
- Stop it! I don't want to hear about the problem I left out. I knew the rest of the test!
- I choose to remember the compliments I got.
- I deserve that compliment. I do look well today.
- Voice, you're only looking for rejection.
- So what if I got points taken off for not parking exactly in the middle of the space. I passed the driving test!
- So what if Greta Grumper doesn't like me. There are lots of people who do!
- There's more to life than catching fly balls.

Remember to look for the positive when the Voice is filtering. If it is pointing out your failures, have your Back Talk stress your successes. When the Voice tells you the little things you did wrong, tell it the things you did right. Whatever negative the Voice comes up with, you can counter with a positive. At first it may take a while to become aware of the positive side of things because you've been listening to negatives from the Voice for a long time.

To make your Back Talk most effective, make a list of positive comments you receive. Beside each positive comment, write the name of the person who gave it to you. Keep your list in a place where you can look at it several times a day. Put it on the mirror in your room so you see it when you comb your hair. Tape it on a door in your room. Put it in your notebook. When the Voice starts with the negative comments, you can use your list of positives to talk back, and you can tell the Voice who else agrees with you.

On another paper make a list of what you do well. The Voice will try to convince you that you're being conceited or that what you're writing is no big deal, but make your list anyway. Whenever you receive a compliment about something you do well, put it on both your lists. Update your lists daily, and keep them over a long period of time. The longer you keep the list, the less filtering your Voice will get away with as time goes on.

Overgeneralizing

You know the Voice is overgeneralizing when it uses *always, never, everybody, nobody, any, every, none, all*. Some favorite Voice expressions of overgeneralization are "Why can't you ever...," "How come you never...," "Will you never learn...," "You know you always...," "Everybody's going to...," "Nobody will ever...," "Any two-year-old could...."

When you back-talk the Voice's overgeneralizations, pay

special attention to making more specific, balanced statements. Disagree with the Voice and add your balanced view.

BACK TALK FOR OVERGENERALIZATION

- I don't *always* mess up. Sometimes I do, but most times I don't.
- A few people may not like what I do.
- Two-year-olds are not capable of doing this better than I do it.
- The team will get off the field even though I'm out here.
- Only a few people are involved, not everybody.
- Stop telling me what I *always* do. Most of the time I handle this very well.
- Don't tell me I'll never learn. This is my first try, and I'll get better with practice.
- Four lines is not a simple phone system, and I *can* work it.
- Just because I don't have a date for the Junior Prom doesn't mean I'll never go out on a date again.
- Not having a boyfriend now doesn't mean I'll never have a boyfriend.
- Stop overgeneralizing!
- I know you're overgeneralizing. Voice, and I'm not buying it. Bug off!

Choose some Back Talk from the list to use as a pattern to write your own Back Talk for your Voice's favorite overgeneralizations. Then pick the strongest ones to memorize. When the Voice starts peppering you with *always, never, everybody, nobody,* you'll be ready with positive support for yourself.

Mind Reading

If your Voice has been participating in the great American pastime of mind reading, you're going to have to be very forceful in your Back Talk to stop it. Whenever the Voice assumes that someone is thinking negatively about you, give the person the benefit of the doubt. Here is some general Back Talk for mind reading.

BACK TALK FOR MIND READING

- There's no way to know what they're thinking.
- Don't assume!
- I can't believe that before I check it out.
- He probably *isn't* thinking that.
- What she thinks is none of my business.
- The only way I can know is to ask.
- You can't guess how someone will feel, Voice.
- She probably thinks I'm okay.
- Stop it!
- Come off it, Voice!

The Back Talk list that Kay Kind developed for mind reading looked like this:

Voice Statements	*Back Talk*
She was probably disgusted.	She said it was okay, and I believe her.
She was just being polite.	I believe Aunt Harri.
I know what she was *really* thinking.	She said what she was thinking.

Voice Statements	Back Talk
She was trying to make you feel better.	Drop it, Voice, I'm not listening.
Those two women are going to be furious.	You don't know how they will feel.
It's obvious how they'll feel.	You can't predict how people will feel.
Of course, I can.	Baloney! Get lost!
They'll probably tell Aunt Harri to fire you.	Stop it, Voice! They'll probably understand.
You hope they'll understand.	Shut up, Voice! The discussion is over!

When the Voice is mind reading, it is especially important that you remember NEVER to agree with it. As in everything else, the Voice ALWAYS lies.

Awfulizing

The Voice will keep you in a state of anxiety if you listen to its "What ifs." The awful catastrophes that the Voice implies will surely happen are not life-threatening even though it tells you, "You'll die if that happens." It's simple to back-talk the Voice when it's awfulizing; however, it's not easy to follow through with the action that it's stopping. Give yourself the permission and the support to get "unstuck" from the Voice's awfulizing by saying, "Even if."

BACK TALK FOR AWFULIZING

- It's okay to go ice skating even if I look stupid.
- It's okay to give my report even if it's boring.
- It's okay to ask for her phone number even if she might not give it to me.

- I'll live even if I miss the ball and the boys are watching.
- I'll have a good time even if I don't have a date.
- It's okay to ask for a date even if she turns me down.
- I'm okay even if I can't catch fly balls.
- I'm okay even if I feel embarrassed.
- It's okay to put in an application even if I don't get the job.
- It's okay to try out for the team even if I have to sit on the bench.
- It's okay to take my driving test even if I might not pass it.
- It's okay to talk to someone I don't know even if she might not want to talk to me.

Whatever you may feel embarrassed about, fearful of, stupid over, you are okay regardless. The catastrophes of the Voice cannot keep you from being a good person or doing whatever you want to do unless you allow it. Give yourself permission to enjoy life and yourself!

Be Perfect

If your Voice is very busy pushing you to be perfect or reminding you that you're not perfect, you need to give yourself lots of supportive permission to be an ordinary human being. With the Voice telling you that you are either a 1 or a 10, it's very important to let the Voice know that 2 through 9 count and that you're going to accept less than 10 as okay.

Voice Messages	Back Talk
You really messed up this time.	It's okay to make a mistake.

Voice Messages	*Back Talk*
You were lucky to get credit for that.	It's okay if it wasn't perfect.
Look how wrinkled your shirt is.	It's okay if it doesn't stay perfect all day.
Do that over, you made a mistake.	It's okay to leave a mistake.
You could have done better.	It's okay to choose to do less than my best.
You're so careless.	It's okay to make a mistake.
You'd better do more so you'll be best.	It's okay if I'm not number one. 2 through 9 count.
You hurt her feelings.	It's okay to be human. I didn't hurt her on purpose.

To fight the Voice's Be Perfect effectively, you have to be on guard as well for the sneaky messages that are buried in other messages. Any time you feel "less than" or "not enough," look for the Be Perfect message and give yourself permission to have a 4 or a 6 or an 8 instead of a 10. Sometimes 2 is very good. If you've never skied before and you make it down the hill with only three falls instead of ten, you've definitely improved! Your skiing may still be a 2, but it's okay to have a 2 your first time out. Your Voice will say that you look stupid, but it's okay to fall down when you're learning to ski. You can't be perfect, so don't give it a worry! Tell the Voice to "Buzz off!" and get on with the fun.

Any time you are learning a new skill, the Voice will demand perfection. Pretend that you are supporting a friend in learning something new and be as supportive to yourself as you would be to your friend. Allow yourself the right to be a human being, expect imperfection, and get okay with making mistakes. Choose to do the best you can and even to accept less than your best when it suits you.

Accept for yourself that 2 through 9 count and decide when
a 7 is as good as you're going to make it. It won't be easy if
your Voice is pushy with Be Perfect, but you can do it by
being supportive of your Inner Being who is so very beau-
tifully, imperfectly human.

Guilt Trips

Guilt trips come from the Voice's "shoulding" on you. It
tells you that you "should" do something or you "shouldn't"
do something; that you "should" have known this or
"should" have said that or "shouldn't" have said something
else. The Voice says you "could" have done one thing and
"have to" do another. All those obligations put on by the
"should" cause you to feel guilty because you can't meet
them.

It is important that you become aware of the "should."
You may not hear it because it has become such a part
of you. Listen for other people "shoulding" on you and
themselves. Before you try to do anything about getting rid
of the "should," become very conscious of how common it
is in your conversation and that of others.

To relieve yourself of the dominating "should" of the
Voice, substitute "I choose/don't choose to" or "I want/
don't want to."

BACK TALK FOR GUILT TRIPS

"You should at least have got her phone number."
　　I chose not to get her phone number.
"You should have started sooner."
　　I chose not to start sooner, and I accept the conse-
　　quences of that choice.
"You should have stayed right where you were."

I chose not to stay right where I was, and I accept the consequences of that choice.

"You should call Polly."

I want to call Polly.

"You should do your homework now."

I want to do my homework now.

"You should not forget to take your coat when you go to the game."

I want to remember my coat when I go to the game.

Back Talk for "shouldn't" is different from "should" because there is a "You're not okay" or a "Be Perfect" message as well as the guilt. Talking back to "shouldn't" requires an "I'm okay" message as well as acknowledgment of your choice.

BACK TALK FOR "SHOULDN'T"

"You shouldn't say you hate your brother."

Right now I feel hate, and I choose to express it. It's okay to feel my feelings.

"You shouldn't be mad at your mother."

Right now I feel anger because I think my mother is being unfair. It's okay to feel angry.

"You shouldn't be late to class."

It's okay to be late because I was with my counselor. I chose to talk to Mark instead of being on time. I'm willing to accept the consequences of my decision. If I'm late, I accept the responsibility.

"How could you forget?" (You shouldn't forget.)

I'm human, and human beings forget important things sometimes. It's okay if I'm not perfect.

"You should have been more careful." (You shouldn't be careless.)

Sometimes I make mistakes. It's okay to make a mistake.

There are times when your behavior is inappropriate, and you feel uncomfortable about it. In order to feel good about yourself, you need to make amends for your behavior. In those cases it's important that you go directly to the person or persons involved and make amends, and it must be done in a way that is meaningful to both of you. Sometimes it may be a simple apology. Other times you may feel the need to do more. If you broke your neighbor's window, you need to pay for the window. The amends you make should reflect the significance or degree of the wrong.

Watch out for the Voice's nagging you to make amends when it is unnecessary and not your responsibility. Wendy's Voice wanted her to phone Polly and arrange to meet her for lunch the next day. Wendy wasn't the only one who didn't save a place for Polly, but Wendy's Voice wanted her to take full responsibility. If you're constantly apologizing for everything, your Voice is putting total responsibility for the running of the world on you. Forget it! You need to sort out what's yours and what belongs to others. A little self-assertion is in order!

As you go over your list of "shoulds," note the ones that the Voice uses most frequently. Write strong statements of choice and support for those and work on catching the Voice and talking back every time it "shoulds" on you.

You're Not Okay

You're Not Okay is a very sneaky message sent by the Voice because it seldom comes right out and says it, but you *feel* it. When you have the feeling that you're rotten, no good, not good enough, not smart enough, not anything enough, the Voice is saying, "You're not okay." It's often hidden in other messages. Larry's Voice said, "What makes you think she could like you anyway?" What a sneaky way to say, "You're not good enough. Something's wrong with you."

Much of the time You're Not Okay is part of Be Perfect or Guilt Trips. "You shouldn't be so careless," causes guilt and also sends the message, "You made a mistake. You're not perfect." "Why can't you ever do anything right?" is an overgeneralization that says, "You're not perfect," and makes you feel not good enough. It gives you a big You're Not Okay.

Fighting You're Not Okay is very difficult until you separate what you do from who you are. You are an okay person no matter what you do. Some of your behavior may be inappropriate and in need of change. You are an okay person. Your worth does not depend on what you do. You are an important and worthwhile person. The Voice will tell you that you must be perfect to be worthwhile. That is pure garbage, and the Voice needs to be told so!

BACK TALK FOR YOU'RE NOT OKAY

- I'm okay even if I make a mistake.
- I'm okay even if I'm not perfect.
- I'm good enough just the way I am.
- My worth doesn't depend on what I do.
- My worth doesn't depend on how I look.
- My worth doesn't depend on your approval.
- It's okay to do the best I can.
- It's okay to make a mistake.
- I'm okay even if I forgot my notes.

- No matter what I do I'm okay.
- I'm an okay person just because I'm alive.
- I'm okay no matter what my feelings are.
- I'm okay even if I'm criticized by others.
- I'm okay even if I have big feet.
- It's okay for me to take my time.
- It's okay for me to be a beginner.
- I'm okay even if someone is angry with me.
- I'm okay even if I'm overweight.
- I'm okay even if I'm skinny.
- I'm okay even if I got a C.
- I'm okay even if I didn't win.
- I'm okay even if I won't win a beauty contest.
- I'm okay even if nobody else likes me.
- I'm okay and I like me.
- I like me because I am worthwhile and important.
- I'm okay because I'm a human being.
- I'm okay because I'm me.
- I'm okay just because I'm okay!

Catch your sneaky Voice when it's telling you you're not okay and bombard it with your I'm Okay messages. Write at least ten of your own. Each day choose one I'm Okay message that you've written to be your affirmation of the day. Say it to yourself all day. Write it at least ten times during the day. No matter what messages the Voice sends you, say your I'm Okay message. It will give you something to distract the Voice until you get your Back Talk organized against a specific attack by the Voice.

When you have your eight papers or cards completed with your Voice messages on one half and your Back Talk beside them, you're ready to talk back to the Voice. You won't win every battle with the Voice, but if you keep at it you will build your inner support system until the Voice is a minor pest in your life. As you build your support from within, you'll be able to accept the positive regard of others. You won't *need* their approval, but you'll be able to receive it because your critical Voice won't be there to reject it.

Now that you know how your Voice holds you back, it's time to get in touch with your Inner Being, that beautiful, positive, supportive part of you that is blocked and pushed aside by the Voice. Your Inner Being is where your true feelings are. To have your true feelings acknowledged, accepted, and valued, you must be able to share them with others. To protect the rights of your Inner Being you must have a way to stand up for yourself. Through assertiveness you can protect your rights and share your true feelings.

CHAPTER 7

Values and
Self-esteem

Wishing she could become invisible. Corinne Cordial stood in line at the theater with Monty Monotonous. She had hoped that no one she knew would be there, but as she looked around it seemed that everyone she knew was there. This was really awful. She hadn't wanted to go out with Monty, but when he asked her she couldn't refuse and hurt his feelings. It wasn't that Monty was so bad; he just wasn't so good. Corinne liked him all right as a friend at school. He sat across from her in chemistry lab, and they would talk while they were doing experiments. She didn't know that he thought she was interested in him just because she talked to him in chemistry. When he asked her to go to the movie, she was totally surprised and didn't know how to get out of it. So here she was feeling embarrassed to be seen on a date with Monty.

Doing what she didn't want to do wasn't new to Corinne. People were always asking favors, and she didn't know how to say no. She felt trapped a lot of the time. Her Voice would tell her that to be a good friend she should do what her friends asked her to do. Corinne was hung up on, "What will they think if you say no?" It always seemed that she was doing things she didn't want to do. She was always putting other people before herself. Her Voice told her that was what she should do, but she couldn't help feeling resentful about always being the one to do favors.

At the day-care center where she worked Corinne would stay to wait for a father who was late almost every Wednesday. It was the only day he picked up his son, and he knew that six o'clock was closing time. The man would breeze in ten to twenty minutes late, say a hurried, "Sorry I'm late," and never thank Corinne for staying with his son. Trina Totlot, the owner of the center, would be working in the office and wouldn't notice when the man came in. Corinne really wanted Trina to tell the man to pick up his son on time, but she didn't want to say anything that might make waves. She wished Trina would notice when he was late. Several times Corinne had gone into the office and said, "Well, Mr. Laggard finally got here." Most of the time Trina would give Corinne an absentminded "Thanks for staying," say good-bye, and go right on with her work.

Corinne knew that she didn't have to stay, but it made it possible for Trina to get her book work done and get home sooner. Nobody would have to stay if Trina would remind Mr. Laggard of the overtime rule and tell him that he had to pick up Leon by six or pay overtime. Overtime was 50 cents a minute. The five dollar late charge for ten minutes would help remind Mr. Laggard to be on time. Corinne wished Trina would talk to Mr. Laggard.

With a sigh of resignation, Art Affable got into the car. He hadn't wanted to stay at this party in the first place.

When he got here and found that everyone was doing coke and smoking pot, he wanted to leave. Art didn't mind if people were drinking. Everyone knew that he didn't drink and accepted it, so no one bugged him about that. Tonight it really made him mad when Rudy Goash kept trying to get him to take a hit off a bong.

Going to this party had been Brad Brasher's idea, and that was another thing that bothered Art. When he asked Allan Apt and Dan Dawdle if they wanted to go out since he had the car this weekend, he didn't know that they'd invite Brad to go along too. Art didn't want to be around Brad. The last time he'd gone out and Brad has been in the group, Brad had gotten drunk and rowdy and Art had been embarrassed. Now here he was embarrassed again because Brad had made a fool of himself and everyone knew that Brad was riding with him. They would all think Brad was his friend. He wanted to tell Dan and Allan what he thought about their inviting Brad to go along, but he knew he wouldn't do that. They might get mad if he did.

While she was standing in front of the school waiting for her dad to pick her up, Felicia Fetching had overheard a conversation between Connie Jeanial and Sherman Sharp. They had been discussing something that had happened the weekend before, and Felicia couldn't get the conversation out of her mind. It wasn't that it was about anything particularly important. It was the way Connie stood up for her convictions. Sherman had disagreed with Connie when she'd said that it was inconsiderate, immature, and minor vandalism to throw toilet paper all over the trees and bushes in front of houses. Sherman had said it was just for fun and everybody was having a good time. He'd said Connie was a nerd for not joining in. Connie had said, "I'm not a nerd. I won't do something I think is stupid just because everybody else is doing it."

Felicia was sure that if she'd been with the group she would have been throwing toilet paper. She wouldn't even have thought about it; she would've just done it. She knew she wouldn't have stood up to Sherm the way Connie did. She couldn't help feeling admiration for Connie, and she wished she could be more like her.

Self-esteem is more than just liking yourself. It's an attitude of acceptance without judging. It's a feeling of personal competence and personal worth; a feeling that you are a capable person in your world and deserve to be treated well and receive good in your life. It's a feeling of having value, of being important.

To feel valuable and important you must know what there is about you that is of value or importance. You must know what you value and what is important to you. To Connie Jeanial, consideration for others was of importance. She valued that; and she had to stand up for that value when she was out with her friends and later when she was talking with Sherman. If you have spent your whole life listening to others and your Voice, you may not know what is of value to you or about you. You could have accepted the values and opinions of others without testing and evaluating them to see if they're beliefs that make sense to you.

How Values Are Formed

Your beliefs and values that determine how you cope with your world came to you the same way your beliefs about yourself did. Originally you accepted and adopted the beliefs of your parents because doing so gave you security and approval. Your parents judged people's behavior and then labeled it with words such as honest, hard-working, dependable, responsible, brave, thoughtful, dishonest, irresponsible, cowardly, weak, lazy, or stupid. You accepted those labels and judgments about yourself and others, and you applied them to situations in your life. You learned how people are "supposed to" handle their anger, sadness, joy, anxiety, and other emotions. You learned the "right way" to do things, what were "okay" subjects to talk about, what you "shouldn't" talk about, what your "duty" was to your family, what behavior was acceptable at home and in public, and what your goals in life "should" be. Accepting those values and beliefs assured you of safety and security in your family.

In order to feel safe and secure outside your home, you took on the values and beliefs of others who were important to you. While staying at a friend's house you may have learned that you're "supposed to" bow your head and say grace before meals. Since your family didn't do that, you didn't know about it, but from then on, at that friend's house, you adopted their value about saying grace before meals and bowed your head.

Adults you respected or who had authority or influence over you gave you many of your rules, beliefs, and values. As time went on, your need to feel secure and safe with your peers caused you to adopt their values and disregard or forget some of the values of significant adults. To be accepted by your peers you took on their rules about how to act with the opposite sex, what your "duty" is to your family and others, how you "should" dress, feel, and behave, and how you "should" react to adults. Sometimes peers offer a "package deal," and you are required to accept everything whether or not you agree with everything. Part of the package is that you *never* say what you feel uncomfortable about.

Most of the things that you judge good or bad, acceptable or unacceptable, right or wrong, okay or not okay have to do with your being approved of by others. If you like to wear white slip-on sneakers but everyone else is wearing black high-top sneakers with Velcro fasteners, you may not want to wear what you like because of the reaction of others. When the crowd goes out to TP a house, you may be like Felicia and go along without thinking because "everybody's doing it." Or you might have some feelings about it but go along because your Voice says, "They won't want you around if you don't join in."

Being approved of is of vital importance, and the values of your peer group can sometimes be in conflict with the values of your home. At those times the choice between approval from your peers and approval from your family can cause you much pain. Whose approval is more important? Whose disapproval will it be easier to live with? Your choice is between bad and worse, or so it seems. Actually, you have a third choice—your own approval.

Developing Your Own Values

Deciding what *you* believe, what *you* value, what is important to *you* takes careful thought and evaluation. It takes time and effort to develop rules that you're willing to stand by because *you* feel they are best for you. It takes strength and courage to stand by your values when your peers challenge you on them. Felicia Fetching admired Connie Jeanial for standing up for her beliefs. Connie decided she didn't want to be involved in the "toilet paper caper" and was willing to take the disapproval of the group. Her own approval was more important to her.

During the teen years it's natural to pull away from your parents, but some teens go overboard and reject all the rules, beliefs, and values of their parents. It's not unusual to hear a teen say, "I just don't have the same values as my parents. They want everything their way and won't consider my values at all." Usually that can be translated to, "I've accepted the values of my peer group and think my parents are stupid and old-fashioned. If they won't see things my way, it's just too bad. I'm not doing things their way." Accepting the values of one group doesn't mean you must reject all the values of the other.

Placing value judgments of right and wrong on matters of taste or preference causes conflict between adults and teens. It seems that some adults want teens to conform to their ideas of how teens "should" look and act, and if teens don't look and act that way they're judged as worthless or bad. Some teens behave irresponsibly and inconsiderately and don't treat others with dignity and respect. Then they get pushed out of shape when they're confronted about their unacceptable behavior. There's a happy medium in there someplace.

If you treat others with dignity and respect and behave in a dignified, self-respecting way, what you wear or how you cut your hair won't be such an issue. Look at your motive behind insisting on a particular haircut, style or color of clothing, jewelry, or music. Do you value the approval of your peers so much that you're willing to alienate your parents? Is your need to be independent from your parents so great that you're willing to be in constant conflict with them? Is it so important to have your own way that you won't compromise with adults on any issue? Are you so intent on being part of the group that you accept values that have negative effects on you?

If those questions make you feel uncomfortable or angry,

you may well be ignoring your Inner Being. Your Inner Being is that feeling deep inside that lets you know when things aren't just right. The Voice in your head is telling you to ignore that feeling, but you know it's there. If you're in conflict with your parents, no matter whom you blame, *you* don't feel good. It's time to look at your values, and you may need help to do that. Talking things over with your friends is usually not a reliable way to explore value conflicts with your parents because friends generally agree with you and you get nowhere. You need a trusted adult to give you feedback and suggestions on how to discuss your differences with your parents. Your school counselor, a friend's mother or father, an aunt or uncle, a teacher you trust, a minister or priest, an older brother or sister, or a private counselor are people who can help you. Some of your classes in school may offer opportunities to explore your values. Knowing what your values are and that they fit you makes it possible for you to live by them.

Values Affect Self-esteem

Felicia Fetching could admit to herself that she would have gone along with the crowd and thrown toilet paper. Because of overhearing the conversation between Connie and Sherm, Felicia began to explore her values about going along with the gang no matter what. Since Felicia is part of a youth group at church, she'll probably have an opportunity to talk about it there and decide what she values and how she will deal with such situations in the future.

When Art realized that there was drug use going on it made him uncomfortable. His Inner Being was letting him know that he didn't belong there. However, his Voice told him that he "couldn't" leave because his friends wanted to stay. Art had a choice, but he didn't think he did. Leaving early with or without his friends was rejected because he didn't want them to get mad or think he was being stupid. What was going on at the party was against his values, but he stayed anyway and lost self-esteem as a result. Because he thought others would consider him to be Brad's friend, Art lost more self-esteem when he felt he would be connected to Brad's behavior, which was not up to his standards and values.

Corinne Cordial's Inner Being let her know that going out with Monty would be a mistake, but her Voice told her that she "shouldn't" refuse because Monty might be hurt. Corinne placed more value on how Monty would feel than on her own feelings and failed to follow her Inner Being. As a result she felt bad about herself for going out with Monty. Ignoring her Inner Being cost her some self-esteem.

Being considerate and helping friends was an important value to Corinne. She often did what she didn't want to do because it would make someone else feel good. She allowed Trina and Mr. Laggard to take advantage of her because she didn't want to "make waves." While all this being a good friend and a considerate person was going on, Corinne's Inner Being gave her a message of discomfort. Because she didn't listen to her Inner Being, Corinne began to feel resentful toward others. Her Voice kept telling her that she "should" be a good friend and she "shouldn't" feel the way she did. The conflict came because Corinne valued being kind to others, but she also valued others' being kind to her and not taking advantage of her. When she allowed others to take advantage to her, she lost some self-esteem.

Connie Jeanial's Inner Being let her know that she wasn't comfortable about TPing a house, and she listened to it and refused to participate. She felt good about standing up for that value and gained some self-esteem. She maintained her self-respect because she satisfied her own standards and values rather than those of the group.

Behaving according to your values keeps you feeling good about yourself. Accepting your choices and being responsible to yourself for the consequences of them is a way of behaving in accordance with your values. Looking inside yourself for your self-worth instead of seeking approval from outside will help you make the choices that will keep you centered on what you believe and value. Staying in harmony with the values of your Inner Being builds and maintains your self-esteem. Anytime you do anything that ignores or disregards your Inner Being, you lessen your self-esteem.

Message That Confuse

Because you don't get straight messages, it is sometimes difficult to determine your values and the values of those around you. If parents say that honesty is an important value, and when the phone rings they tell you to say they're not at home, it's hard to know what they really believe. Political events like the Iran-Contra Affair where almost the entire executive branch of the government was under investigation and everyone involved was pointing fingers and blaming everyone else make you wonder what the government of this country stands for. When a man like TV evangelist Jim Bakker, who represents himself as a servant of God, is involved in a sex scandal, it makes you wonder what religion is all about.

In every case of unethical behavior by politicians, religious leaders, entertainers, and other public figures who lose the respect and esteem of people can be seen the violation of a belief or value that is held by the people. Many times the original misdeed pales in importance to events that come later. Jim Bakker did something very human but against the values of those who followed him. The cover-up and payoff of the woman who was involved became important to people who weren't much interested in his sexual behavior. When Senator Gary Hart's liaison with a woman not his wife was revealed by the Miami *Herald*, his first reaction was to try to minimize the relationship and virtually lie his way out. The American public didn't buy the lie because further evidence confirmed the association. Again, the outrage for some was more for the attempt to cover up than for the deed itself.

How can you explain the difference between the outcry regarding Bakker and Hart and the nation's reaction to Oliver North? Lieutenant Colonel Oliver North became a folk hero because of his dash and derring-do before a Congressional committee, but he admitted lying and shredding documents that would have been incriminating to himself and others. Besides keeping his illegal activities hidden from Congress, he used secret funds to purchase personal items, accepted a $16,000 security system as an illegal gift and forged letters to cover it up, and denied knowledge of a $200,000 trust fund that had been set up as an insurance policy for his family by Albert Hakim. In a *Newsweek* magazine poll taken on July 9 and 10, 1987, 65 percent of those polled said that North was well-meaning but did things that were illegal. Of those polled, 70 percent said that he should not be indicted and tried on criminal charges. Obviously, being faithful to one's wife is more valued by the ordinary American than being honest and ethical in government. Wheeling and dealing at high government levels is outside the day-to-day life of the average American, but being faithful to your mate is very real to everyone.

Further uproar arose in the Bakker scandal when it was

discovered that Jim Bakker and his wife, Tammy, were living in opulent luxury on the money collected through his television ministry. The money was not being used to do God's work as the contributors supposed, but was providing Jim and Tammy with a life-style that was unreachable and inconceivable to the trusting people who sent the money. After the excesses of the Bakkers were revealed, many people said they still would support the Bakkers and their ministry, while others were outraged. The different responses reflect the differing values of people.

Not every American condemned Bakker and Hart or approved of Ollie North. Editorial pages across the nation were filled with letters expressing differing points of view. Learning to live with differences is an important part of getting along in the world and in the family. It becomes more complicated when you receive differing views in the same message, as you do with, "Honesty is the best policy, but business is business." You have to make some important decisions then. What does being honest mean to you? Do you expect other people to be honest with you all the time? Are you honest with others all the time? When is it okay not to be honest? Is it okay to steal from the government or a large corporation but not from ordinary people? Are your standards of honesty consistent? Do you live up to your standards of honesty?

Standing Up for Your Values

With conflicting messages all around you, it's difficult to know what to do. When friends have different views on issues, it's hard to take a stand. Art Affable was able to go to the party and not drink or use drugs, but he couldn't tell his friends he wanted to leave early. Putting the needs of others before her own needs left Corinne Cordial feeling bad about herself. She had a difficult time because her feelings told her that she was upset because others took advantage of her, and her Voice told her that she "should" be a good friend.

The key to standing up for what you believe in is being assertive, and it is one of the most important ways you can support your self-esteem. Much of the time you undermine your own self-esteem because you don't deal with yourself assertively. When the conflict between you and the Voice begins, you don't know how to fight the Voice. Art did okay with the drug issue because he had very strong feelings about it, but when he thought of leaving the party the Voice said, "They'll be mad if you leave early. Everybody's going to think you're being stupid." Because he wanted approval from his peers, Art chose not to leave, but he didn't feel good about himself for staying. He needed to be assertive with himself to support his self-esteem.

In addition to dealing with yourself assertively, it's important that you learn to deal with others assertively. Standing up for what you believe enhances your self-esteem, and expressing your feelings effectively gives you a feeling of power in your world. To be assertive is to treat yourself and others with dignity and respect. It is to protect your Inner Being from being harmed by others or by the critical Voice in your head that stops you from appreciating the very special person you are.

CHAPTER ◇ 8

Self-awareness;
the Bridge to
Self-assertion

With a big sigh Peggy Pleezer hung up the phone
and wrote "track meet" on the calendar. She had
planned to go shopping with Trisha Trendy
on Saturday, but Coach Swift was in a bind for a timer at
the track meet, and Peggy just couldn't let him down. He
hadn't asked her to do Saturday meets this year, but since
Jenni Jentry had the flu, he really didn't have anyone
else to help. Shopping with Trisha would have been fun
because Trisha had such good style, but it was no big
deal.

Before the phone rang, Peggy had been thinking about
the rally at school the day before. She'd been on the
decorating committee and had made some big tissue paper
flowers to add color to the gym. The committee had told
Peggy that she could keep the flowers, but when she went

to get them after the rally she saw Ima Imposer walking out with them. She'd wanted to stop Ima and tell her that the flowers weren't for just anybody to take, but she decided it wasn't worth the hassle. Even though Peggy had spent a lot of time on the flowers because she'd planned to put them in her room in a vase she'd made in caramics class, her Voice told her it wasn't that important. She'd just try to find time and money to make some more.

The sound of the door slamming made Barry Belligerent feel good. He'd feel better if he could hit something. He was so mad he wanted to tear something apart. The wooden planks of the porch grumbled in protest under his thundering feet as he strode furiously from the house. He was sick of being called a hoodlum and a bum because he wore a black leather jacket and rode a motorcycle. Some motorcycle—an old Honda that was so beat up when he got it that the guy was embarrassed to take fifty dollars for it. Barry had been willing to pay fifty for it because the frame was worth at least that. He'd rebuilt the whole bike from one end to the other, and every cent he'd put into it he'd earned himself.

Barry had worked on the bike for three months before it was ready to ride, and the whole time his father had been on his back. All he'd heard was, "Only hoodlums ride motorcycles"; "I don't want my son roaring around town like a hood making me look bad"; "That thing will bring nothing but trouble"; "You just want to take up with that tough motorcycle gang over on Front Street." Barry had come close to throwing a wrench at his father more than once.

When he'd first started working on the bike, Barry had not been interested in getting involved with any club, group, or gang, but the more his father hassled him the more attractive the idea seemed, especially after what happened tonight. Barry was putting on his new leather jacket that had taken three months of saving to buy, and his father had come up and grabbed the front of the jacket and screamed in his face that if he was going to dress like a hood and go around with hoods he was not welcome in this house. As he jumped on his bike and roared off, Barry was thinking that joining a club would be a good way to get even with his father.

Exhausted from crying, Trisha Trendy decided to go wash her face and do her homework. She had come home from school feeling horrible because Mr. Zero had humiliated her in front of the class by asking her how she could look so put together and be so scatterbrained in math. After class Rick Romeo had told her he didn't care what kind of brain she had as long as she looked the way she looked. Trisha had wanted to tell Rick that she didn't appreciate his condescending attitude, but she had started to cry before she could get a word out. Rick had patted her on the shoulder and told her that what Zero said didn't matter anyway. Trisha had walked away feeling frustrated and upset.

When she got home, Trisha told her mother what happened, and her mother said, "You're too sensitive, Trisha. Rick was just trying to cheer you up. He didn't mean anything by it." Trisha tried to tell her mother how put down she felt, but her mother insisted that it was nothing to get upset about. Finally, in frustration, Trisha had burst into tears, rushed to her room, and thrown herself on the bed, but not before hearing her mother say, "I don't know why she gets hurt so easily."

As soon as she walked in the door, Glenna Gleemer knew something was wrong. She could just feel it. With a smile and a cheery "Hi, Mom," Glenna tried to get through the kitchen and into the hall, but her mother stopped her with, "Glad to see somebody around here's in a good mood." Knowing she was caught, Glenna decided to get an apple and sit down while her mother told her how bad things had been today. It meant about fifteen minutes of being cheerful and understanding when she really wanted to scream, "Why can't you ever have a good day? Why can't you ever ask me what kind of day I've had?"

Nobody asked Glenna what kind of day she was having because, looking at her, everyone assumed she was having a great day. No matter what happened, Glenna always had a smile on her face. If something made her angry and she talked about it to friends, she smiled the entire time she was telling her story. When she walked down the hall, she smiled. While she sat in class, she smiled. When she told Stephanie Stable about her mother, Glenna's eyes were sad but her mouth smiled. Telling how hurt she was by Rudy Goash's put-downs didn't change the smile on Glenna's face. Even when she cried, Glenna smiled.

Feelings

Feelings are part of being human. Everyone has feelings, but most people aren't aware of the full range of their feelings. Barry Belligerent feels little besides anger. Glenna Gleemer tries not to feel at all but allows herself to look happy most of the time. The feelings of others are very important to Peggy Pleezer, but she ignores her own feelings. When she's feeling angry, Trisha Trendy cries.

Most of the time people communicate ideas but not feelings. Rick Romeo might say, "I think Mr. Zero is a jerk," but he's not going to say, "I feel uncomfortable when Mr. Zero puts people down because I know that I'd feel humiliated if anyone did that to me." Generally, people cover up their true feelings because they're afraid of what others might think or they fear the reactions of others. When his father berated him and called him a hood, Barry couldn't say, "I feel hurt when you put me down like that." He didn't want his father to know how terrible he felt, so he covered it up with anger instead.

Feelings get covered, ignored, denied, misinterpreted, and misunderstood because of critical judgments by others and the Voice. When you were a baby and you felt any discomfort, you cried, and someone took care of it. If no one took care of it soon enough, you became angry, cried your angry cry, and people knew you were angry. At the time, you had no Voice in your head telling you that you "shouldn't" be angry. If someone around you thought it wasn't "nice" to be angry, you didn't get that message, and you didn't care. You felt your feelings and communicated them in goo's, giggles, cries, and a variety of sounds, expressions, and behaviors.

Within a short time, infants and toddlers learn what behavior and feelings are acceptable. By the time you were five, you knew whether anger was okay in your house. You had already stopped most of your crying if sadness and hurt were not allowed to be expressed that way. You knew what feelings were acceptable because your family said things such as: "Don't be a baby." "Crying about it won't make it better." "No sense crying over spilt milk." "All you ever do is bawl. Can't you shut up!" "That's no way to come into a room. Go out and come back in with a smile." "You don't hate your brother. Now say you love him."

As you mature, you're given messages about feelings. The messages come from everywhere—parents, relatives, friends, school, TV, church, clubs, radio, neighbors—and they make judgments on feelings. You develop a list of feelings you like and feelings you don't like. You have "yes-yes" feelings and "no-no" feelings. Lists differ according to what is acceptable in your environment. If you come from a home where anger is used to cover up hurt and fear, anger will be on your "yes-yes" list and hurt and fear will be on your "no-no" list. Happy was a "yes-yes" in Glenna's home, but anger or sadness were "no-no's" so Glenna went around looking happy when she wasn't.

The Voice takes over where people leave off, and you then become ruled by the "shoulds" and criticisms of your Voice. When you feel the "no-no" feelings, your Voice says, "You shouldn't feel that way," so you feel guilty about feeling "that way." Then you feel bad about feeling guilty because guilty is usually on the "no-no" list. Most people put sadness on the "no-no" list, and when they feel sad about something, even when it's appropriate, they want to get rid of that "bad" feeling. Barry got rid of sadness by being angry, and Glenna pretended it wasn't there. Many people in our society get rid of their "no-no" feelings by using drugs and alcohol. There's a pill, syrup, tablet, capsule, solution, or elixir advertised that get will rid of any sadness or depression you might be feeling.

Since "yes-yes" feelings are so desirable, you may be like Glenna and pretend to feel happy or glad. After pretending for a long time, you'll lose touch with your true feelings. If you cover your feelings the way Barry and Trisha do, you'll lose your true feelings, and if you take care of everybody else's feelings the way Peggy does, you'll lose your own feelings. If you've been feeling what the Voice has been telling you to feel, you'll need to get in touch with the true feelings of your Inner Being.

In order to discover your feelings, it's necessary to regard them as *facts* without judging them "good" or "bad." Just accept them as being there whether you like them or not. Instead of resisting the feeling the Voice judges as "bad," admit that you feel that feeling. If you do resist, accept your resistance! Tell the Voice, "You bet I'm resisting. I hate this feeling! I don't want to feel this way, but I do. This is really awful!" When you accept the feeling as it is, you'll be able to make decisions about how you want to respond to the feeling. It's not the feeling that's good or bad; it's what you *do* about it that may be good or bad. Feelings just are.

Getting in Touch with Feelings

The Voice and other people have been telling you how you "should" feel, and now it's time to determine and accept how you *do* feel. When you hear the "should" or feel the guilt about the way you are feeling, cancel the "should" and go back to the original feeling before the judgment went on it. What were you feeling before the Voice or person said "should"? That's your true feeling. If you were feeling hatred for your sister, accept that. "Right now I hate my sister." You feel angry and powerless. You wish you didn't have a sister right now. That doesn't mean you're planning to do away with your sister. You may love your sister a lot, but right now she's not so hot. Go ahead and feel your angry feelings.

When you accept your feelings and allow yourself to feel them, you can choose what you plan to do about them. In the matter of feeling angry about something your sister has done, you may choose to express your feelings directly to her in an appropriate, assertive way.

Peggy Pleezer didn't want to time the track meet, but when she felt that she didn't want to help, her Voice said,

"He really needs you. You *should* help." Immediately Peggy felt guilty when she thought of saying no. To avoid the "no-no" feeling of guilt, Peggy agreed to do something she didn't want to do and gave up something that she did want to do. The Voice told her that the coach's needs were more important than hers, so Peggy discounted her own desire to have fun with Trisha and "did her duty." Peggy did that so often that she didn't know what she wanted or how she felt.

When Ima Imposer walked off with the flowers that Peggy had spent so much time and effort making, Peggy's feelings went flat. It was clearly presumptuous and inconsiderate of Ima to walk off with those flowers, and it was certainly appropriate for Peggy to be angry and stop her. Letting it go with an "Oh, well" attitude showed how out of touch Peggy was with her feelings. The acceptance of others as being more important keeps Peggy from knowing her feelings, wants, and needs.

When Peggy felt the "zing" as Ima walked out the door with the flowers, her Inner Being was letting her know that she had feelings about what was going on. When she felt disappointment when the coach called, Peggy had the signal from her Inner Being that all was not well inside, but she ignored it. Ignoring your Inner Being can become so automatic that you tune in to what everyone else feels, wants, and needs and tune out your own Inner Being.

Become aware of the little alarm that your Inner Being sends you. The Voice will want you to ignore it, but allow the feeling to be there. When you know that you're tuned in to your feeling, try to put a label on it. If you tune in to anger or sadness or nothingness, you may need to go further to find out if there's something underneath that you're avoiding. You may need help from someone else to find what's under there. Barry would certainly need a counselor to help him sort through the anger to the hurt, fear, and betrayal that he must feel. Ask for help from others when you need it, because knowing what you feel is important to your self-esteem.

Labeling your feelings can be difficult if you haven't done it very much. Almost everyone can recognize the main categories of mad, glad, and sad; however, there are levels and intensities of feelings that make the categories too broad. The following lists will give you some more specific feeling words to choose from.

Anger	Sadness	Happiness
irritated	dejected	pleased
annoyed	depressed	excited
furious	down	delighted
bugged	unhappy	exhilarated
resentful	gloomy	elated
exasperated	miserable	ecstatic
cranky	crushed	enthusiastic
aggravated	betrayed	thrilled
enraged	defeated	glad
incensed	discouraged	contented

More Feelings		
hopeless	embarrassed	humiliated
desperate	trapped	rejected
put down	disgusted	sorry
worried	anxious	confident
competent	brave	scared
lonely	gratified	comfortable
uncomfortable	loving	trusting
inadequate	attracted	admiring
proud	indifferent	interested
perplexed	undecided	ashamed
eager	overworked	shocked
bored	cautious	frightened

Feelings and Self-esteem

Just as going against your values diminishes your self-esteem, so does ignoring or disregarding your feelings. By discounting your feelings, the unspoken message is, "You're not valuable enough to be listened to. What you feel is not important. Your feelings are wrong. You're not okay." Those are all messages that lessen self-esteem. When Trisha didn't express her anger appropriately and people read her as being "too sensitive," her Voice's message was, "Something's wrong with you." Pleasing others was so important to Peggy that she didn't listen to her true feelings, and she ended up a martyr, carrying the woes of the world on her shoulders, making everything "right" for everyone else but not feeling good about Peggy. The only time she could feel okay was when she was "doing" for someone else, but somehow she always felt walked on by others.

Getting caught up in his own anger kept Barry acting like a thundercloud unleashing bolts of lightning and raining on anything in his path. His true feelings were so frightening to him that he behaved so aggressively that he couldn't respect himself. He couldn't accept his feelings of hurt and degradation, so he struck out at everyone. Being aggressive made him a loser because it kept people away from him. Being friends with someone like Barry is like being friends with an octopus with sore feet. When you step carefully over one foot, you accidentally step on one you didn't see. People like that are always in pain and share their misery with others through their anger. As much as others don't want to be around them, they don't want to be around themselves, and they don't like themselves.

When feelings are ignored or expressed inappropriately, you don't treat yourself with dignity and respect. If you keep your true feelings inside and don't let others know what you really feel, you aren't treating them with dignity and respect either. In order to feel good about yourself, you must treat yourself and others with dignity and respect. You do that by the way you choose to communicate with them.

EXPRESSING FEELINGS

In any encounter with others, you have three choices for expressing your feelings. You can be passive, aggressive, or assertive. To be assertive is to express your feelings honestly, directly, and appropriately in a way that doesn't violate the rights of others. To be aggressive is to express yourself without regard for the rights of others with the purpose of overpowering and dominating. To be passive is to not communicate honestly and directly, to neglect or deny your own feelings, ignore your own rights, and allow others to infringe on them.

Aggressive

Sherman Sharp was sitting at his desk in English before class started, and his foot was in the aisle. Oscar Ordinary walked by and stepped on Sherm's foot.

Sherm: Hey, man, watch where you're goin'.
Oscar: Sorry, Sherm, I didn't see your foot.
Sherm: You blind or somethin', dude? You just messed up my new Reeboks, you nerd.

(Sherm was interested in protecting his own rights without regard for Oscar's. Sherm's only concern was what happened to him, and he didn't care whether Oscar was treated with dignity or respect.)

Passive

Penny Passive was walking toward her car in the mall parking lot when Dommi Neering called to her.

Dommi: Hey, Penny, are you going home now?

Penny: Yeah.

Dommi: Oh, good. Can you give me a ride? I came with Phyllis, but she has to pick up her little brother at day care and won't get home for at least an hour.

Penny: Well, uh...

Dommi: It's only a little bit out of your way, and I'll have more time to get ready for my date if I get home earlier.

Penny: Well, I'm supposed to go right home.

Dommi: It's so close it won't matter, Pen.

Penny: Uh.... Ah.... Well....

Dommi: Gee, thanks, Penny. See you later, Phyllis.

(Penny is so concerned that Dommi might be mad and tell other people how Penny wouldn't give her a ride that she doesn't know what to say. Dommi lives across the freeway from Penny, and it's really inconvenient to take her home, but Penny doesn't know how to say no without feeling that she *should* have said yes. Penny fails to treat herself with dignity and respect and allows others to infringe on her rights.)

Assertive

Melody Moderate was getting ready for school when her sister Merry came into her room.

Merry: Mel, can I borrow your green sweater?
Melody: I just got it back from the cleaners, and I
         don't want to lend it today.
Merry: I'll be real careful with it.
Melody: I don't want to lend it today.
Merry: You know I always take care of your stuff.
Melody: Not today, Merry.
Merry: Maybe can I borrow it later?
Melody: Maybe later.

(Melody stayed with her feeling that she didn't want to
lend her sweater. She didn't allow Merry to infringe on
her right to decide what she would lend and what she
wouldn't. She treated herself and Merry with dignity and
respect.)

When you express your feelings assertively, you take
care of your Inner Being. You say, "I'm important and what
I feel and believe are important." Your feelings are true to
the values of your Inner Being, and when your behavior
isn't in sync with your values, your Inner Being signals
that. When you allow others to take advantage of you and
disregard your rights as Peggy did, you feel uncomfortable
and out of sync with your Inner Being, and that makes you
feel bad about yourself. When you force your will on others
and treat them disrespectfully, you're out of sync with your
Inner Being. Barry's behavior was aggressive, discourte-
ous, and inconsiderate much of the time. His anger ate at
him, and he felt bad about himself. His Voice blamed his
anger and bad feeling about himself on other people, but
buried under that blame and aggressiveness were values
and feelings that were being ignored. It was the betrayal of

his own values and feelings that gave Barry his feelings of low self-esteem.

Important keys to self-esteem are knowing your feelings and being able to express them in an appropriate way. Through assertiveness you can stay true to your values and feelings and share your feelings, wants, and needs with others. You can maintain your self-respect by behaving according to your values, and you can be honest and direct with others without being disrespectful to them.

Being Honest and Direct

Smiling all the time was dishonest of Glenna Gleemer. Her attitude and expression were lies. No one knew who Glenna was, because she hid behind her smile. Glenna was a master player of the great American game, "Guess What I'm Really Feeling." Unfortunately for Glenna, everyone guessed wrong, and that's almost always the outcome of the game. The only way people can know what you're really feeling is for you to tell them in an honest and direct way.

When Rudy Goash offered his put-down comments to Glenna, she needed to let him know that her feelings were hurt, but her Voice told her that she was making something out of nothing. The Voice said, "That's just the way Rudy is. He doesn't mean anything by it." So Glenna smiled and felt put down and began to avoid Rudy. She felt more and more negative toward Rudy and felt uncomfortable when she heard his comments directed at other people. Glenna decided that Rudy was a very uncaring person and wished someone would do something about his cruel comments. It never occurred to Glenna that *she* could do something about them. She had every right to let Rudy know how he affected her, and she could do that in a very gentle way. Without smiling, Glenna needed to say, "It hurts my feeling when I'm called an airhead. I felt it was a put-down." Whenever Rudy makes a comment, Glenna can say, "I felt that was a put-down." Rudy may try to explain it away or tell Glenna she's too thin-skinned. Glenna needn't do anything but stay with her feelings. "I felt it was a put-down." When she does that, she doesn't put Rudy down or get even or infringe on his rights, but she does stand up for herself. She can stop smiling her feelings away.

Expressing anger directly was very difficult for Trisha Trendy. Everyone had to guess what she was feeling, and since she looked so distressed or cried, everyone thought she was sad and hurt. That only made her more frustrated and angry. When Rick made his suggestive comment about her looks, Trisha needed to let him know that she didn't appreciate it. A simple, "I feel insulted by chauvinistic remarks like that," would have taken care of it very nicely. To let Mr. Zero know how she felt about his treatment of her in front of the entire class would take only a moment after class. Going directly to Mr. Zero and stating her feelings in a quiet way would take care of it. "Mr. Zero, I felt humiliated by the sarcastic comment you made during class." Mr. Zero might try to pass it off as a joke, and Trisha need only repeat, "I wanted you to know that I felt humiliated." Trisha could maintain her self-esteem and feel good about herself because she had listened to her Inner Being and been true to herself, her feelings, and her values.

"Guess What I Really Mean" is played with hints and hopes. You do things to give people hints about how you feel and hope they will guess what you're feeling. Trisha hinted to her mother that Rick's behavior bothered her and hoped that her mother would understand. Unfortunately, her mother instead tried to make her feel better and missed Trisha's point entirely. Just as you usually guess wrong when the Voice puts you into mind reading, other people usually guess wrong when you want them to read *your* mind. When you want to be direct, the Voice will try to stop you by saying. "You can't say that. He'll be mad if you do," or "You'll hurt her feelings if you say that." When you're assertive, you treat yourself with diguity and respect, and you don't have to worry about hurt feelings and anger that the Voice has projected for other people. You'll be taking care of your feelings in a way respectful to yourself and others.

Being honest and direct keeps you from being a victim. Peggy didn't share her feelings with Coach Swift and felt taken advantage of. Trisha couldn't find the words to say how angry she was and blamed her mother for misunderstanding her. The comment from Rick made her uncomfortable, but Trisha didn't tell him and felt persecuted. In every case, passiveness caused a feeling of being victimized. Any time you feel like a victim, you are in a state of low self-esteem. You feel out of control of the situation. That helpless, powerless feeling gives the Voice a chance to tell you you're not okay.

By being honest and direct, you state your wants and needs instead of asking questions. You're into "Guess What I Really Mean" when you ask, "Are you hungry?" instead of stating, "I'm hungry." Some people ask, "Are you going to eat all of that?" when they actually mean, "I'd like some of that." If you ask questions instead of stating your wants and needs, you're in for disappointments when people answer your questions with, "No, I had a late lunch," or "Yeah, this is my favorite ice cream, and I can eat a quart with no trouble." Because they didn't guess what you really meant, you loss the game. You don't get your needs met, you feel angry and victimized, and your self-esteem suffers again.

Being honest and direct isn't easy if you've been holding

back and not sharing your true feelings. If you've been ruled by the "should's" of your Voice, you won't trust your true feelings. Trusting your feelings is the basis of self-esteem, and you express those feelings through assertiveness. You have a right to your feelings and are responsible for the expression of them. Allow yourself the open, honest, direct expression of your feelings so you can receive the respect you deserve, and respect others enough to share your true feelings with them. Knowing your values and behaving according to them, and accepting your feelings and expressing them appropriately builds a bridge over the ravine of low self-esteem to the road to high self-esteem.

CHAPTER 9

Building Self-esteem Through Assertiveness

"Well," thought Peggy Pleezer, "here I am again, doing something for somebody that I don't want to do. Why do I always get stuck?" Peggy was selling hot dogs at Debi Dapper's brother's Little League game because Debi had had a tooth pulled and couldn't work today. It was true that Debi was a good friend, but Peggy had worked the track meet last Saturday and had to go to her grandparents' next Saturday, and she was really looking forward to having today to do something fun. When Debi called to ask her to fill in, Peggy couldn't say no. She was feeling trapped and angry with herself for always letting other people take advantage of her, but she didn't know how to say no without hurting their feelings.

• • •

When Mr. Jargon's English classes had to form committees and give reports, Polly Perfect and Harry Hardy had been on the same committee. Being a talented cartoonist, Harry did some dynamite charts to go with the committee's presentation. Polly's job had been to organize the material so Harry could come up with the drawings, and they'd had lots of fun working together. Polly was hoping that Harry would ask her out; he really seemed interested in her, and she had liked him for a long time. After the last committee meeting, Polly had hung around for as long as she could, but Harry had seemed uncomfortable so she left. She was disappointed and wished she'd known some way to let Harry know how she felt, but she was afraid that he'd think she was dumb or, worse yet, pushy.

It was getting harder and harder for Kay Kind to sit at the same table as Greta Grumper at lunch. Besides her constant complaining about everything, lately Greta had started telling Kay what she should do to get Greg Garious to ask her out. The last thing Kay wanted was help from Greta. Greg had been talking to her more and seemed to be working his way up to asking her out. Last week he'd asked her if she'd be going to the basketball game on Friday night and had looked for her and sat in front of her. Kay felt that it wouldn't be long until Greg asked her out, so she wished Greta would just shut up and keep her bad advice to herself or go somewhere else for lunch.

One day after school a bunch of the kids were at the Burger Barn sitting around talking about their favorite videos. Jenni Jentry was part of the crowd, and as the talk got to who had what video, someone asked about the latest from Depeche Mode. Trisha Trendy had seen that one at Jenni's house, so she told everyone Jenni had it. "Not right now," was Jenni's response. "Phyllis borrowed it last week." That brought a groan of sympathy from everyone, because Phyllis Philch was noted for borrowing and taking ages to return anything. Jenni was feeling angry and taken advantage of, but she didn't know how to tell Phyllis she wanted her video back.

Allan Apt was sitting next to Jenni. They had been friends for a long time, and Jenni sometimes helped Allan with his chemistry. Today in class Allan hadn't understood the lecture very well, and he wished Jenni would say something about it. Then he could let her know that he could use some help. He didn't think he could do the assignment alone, but he didn't want to come right out and ask Jenni for help.

Getting Out of Conflict with Yourself

Frustration and a feeling of not being capable of dealing with a situation come as a result of not expressing how you're truly feeling about what's going on. Peggy felt as though everyone were walking all over her, yet she didn't know what to do to stop it. Saying yes when you want to say no puts you in conflict with yourself and lowers your self-esteem. Jenni wanted her video back but didn't know how to ask for it in a way that would be comfortable for her. She was in conflict with herself and felt that "not good enough" feeling. Polly needed to express her positive feelings toward Harry, and Kay needed to express her negative feelings toward Greta. Neither girl knew a way to express her feelings appropriately, and both experienced the frustration of keeping feelings inside, sensing the need to take action but being unable to do so. They felt uncomfortable and inadequate, which results in low self-esteem.

Allan was already feeling inadequate because he didn't understand the chemistry assignment. When he couldn't ask Jenni to help him, he felt even worse. Being unable to express your positive and negative feelings and your wants and needs leaves you unhappy with yourself. Since your feelings are the bridge to self-esteem, and getting in touch with your feelings is so important, you must have a way to assert yourself to share your feelings and values with others. The language of self-assertion begins with the "I" message.

"I" Messages

Stating feelings, wants, and needs honestly and directly can best be accomplished through an "I" message. The feeling words in Chapter VIII are excellent to use in your "I" messages. "I feel irritated when people are late." "I'm glad we had this chance to work together." "I feel exasperated when I study so hard and get a low grade anyway." "I'm angry." "I'm feeling down today." "I resent being called names." "I feel scared." An "I" message is very powerful because it doesn't accuse or criticize anyone else. It stays right with you and you take complete responsibility for yourself and your feelings. On the other hand, a "You" message gives your power away. "You make me mad" says that the other person has control over your feelings. You give away responsibility for your feelings when you say, "You made me feel real bad." It means the other person has the power to make you feel good, and you already know that your good feelings have to come from inside you. When you say, "I feel really crushed about being called sleazy. I don't deserve that," you take responsibility for your own feelings about the other person's behavior without criticizing or judging, and you allow that person to decide what do about that behavior in the future. The judging of the behavior becomes the other person's responsibility.

"I" messages are very powerful, but they're not aggressive. They don't attack or call names. They state your feelings honestly and directly without infringing on the rights of the other person. Stephanie Stable's statement, "I'm furious that my car was full of garbage after our trip to Burger Barn" doesn't attack anyone. If Rita Booker was in the car, she won't feel offended and need to defend herself. She has the opportunity to say, "I understand how you feel. I picked up all my stuff, but I guess some of the other kids didn't. I'll remind them next time." Since she hasn't been accused of anything, she doesn't have any hard feelings, and it isn't necessary for Stephanie to make amends for inappropriate, attacking behavior. If Rita did leave her garbage in the car, she'll have to look at her behavior rather than being on the defensive about Stephanie's. Stephanie keeps her power, and her behavior requires Rita to look at herself.

The "I" message keeps you focused on the problem, and you don't get off on issues that have nothing to do with what happened. With a "You" message Stephanie and Rita could go in a very negative direction.

Steph: You left your garbage in my car and my dad gave me all kinds of heck for it!

Rita: I wasn't the only one in the car. Why don't you tell the others about it?

Steph: I will when I see them.

Rita: Do that. You know, you left your garbage in *my* car the last time I drove.

Steph: I did not! I made sure that I took all my stuff with me when I got out of the car.

Rita: Well, somebody left a mess.

Steph: Well, it wasn't me. Why are you accusing me?

Rita: For the same reason you're accusing me!

Steph: You're really unreasonable, you know, Rita?

Stephanie's upset about the garbage in the car; Rita's upset about being accused and lets Stephanie know that she's upset about the garbage in her car. They're both feeling angry with each other. "You" messages lead to conflict and hard feelings. With "I" messages, conflict and hard feelings can be avoided.

Steph: I'm furious that my car was full of garbage after we went to Burger Barn last Saturday. My dad really got on my case.

Rita: I think I took all my stuff. Next time I'll be sure to get it all.

Steph: I'd really appreciate that.

Since she wasn't accused of the mess, Rita didn't have to be defensive. She took a look at her behavior, decided she may have left some garbage, and offered to be more helpful next time. Stephanie is feeling better because she expressed her negative feelings in an appropriate way and got positive results. "You" messages take the focus off the problem you want to deal with. As soon as Stephanie said, "You left your garbage in my car," Rita was ready to deny it and defend herself. The focus was not on Rita's behavior but had shifted to Stephanie's accusation. Rita wanted to deal with Stephanie's behavior, not her own. To keep focused, use "I" messages.

Some people turn "I" messages into "You" messages. "I feel you're wrong" is a "You" message. Any time you start your sentence with "I feel you..." it is a "You" message. Leave "you" out of the sentence if at all possible. Instead say, "I feel angry about..." or "I feel humiliated when..." Then you'll be talking about what happened, not about the person. Here are some examples of "You" messages turned into "I" messages.

You make me mad.	I feel angry when I'm ignored.
You're wrong.	I disagree.
You're such a slob. You always make a mess.	I feel disgusted when I see peanut butter smeared on the counter top.
You never do anything right.	I feel exasperated when the bread wrapper isn't closed right and the bread gets hard.
You humiliate me.	I feel humiliated.

When you use "I" messages, you keep the focus on your feelings, wants, and needs. Sometimes aggressive people will come back with, "Who cares?" Calmly say, "I just wanted you to know how I feel," and drop it. You've taken care of your feelings. Let the other people think about what you're said. They'll be left with the focus on their behavior, not yours. By using "I" messages you treat others with dignity and respect, avoid infringing on their rights, and respect yourself and your rights in the process.

Expressing Positive Feelings

While Polly and Harry were working on their project, Polly had no trouble telling Harry how great his drawings were. Telling Harry that she enjoyed his sense of humor and appreciated his joking her out of a gloomy mood was another thing. Expressing positive feelings can be as difficult as expressing negative feelings. Aggressive people don't want anyone to think they're "soft" or "mushy," so they hold in their positive feelings. Passive people seldom are in touch with their feelings, or they fail to acknowledge and express any feelings because they're sure that anything they say is unimportant or will be considered stupid.

Americans have idealized the strong, silent man for so long that it's almost un-American for a man to express tender, positive feelings. A boy might be able to tell another boy that he likes his shirt, but it would be almost impossible for him to say, "I'd like to spend more time with you." Girls are allowed to give compliments and say nice things to people. They're even praised for it, but it's rare for anyone to say, "I like you a lot, and I'm glad you're my friend." Think of the times someone has said something like that to you and how good it felt. It's great to be on the receiving end of a positive assertion like that, and it's also great to be on the giving end of it.

By not expressing her positive feelings to Harry, Polly felt frustrated and disappointed. Harry thinks Polly is really cute and lots of fun. She's easy to talk to and he likes being around her, but Harry doesn't know how to express his positive feelings to Polly. He's afraid she'll think he's stupid if he tells her how he feels. Polly and Harry may never got together because neither can express their positive feelings for the other.

In both Polly's and Harry's home, family members don't express their feelings effectively. Since they haven't been shown how to say positive things to others, it's understandable that Polly and Harry keep silent. They're unwilling to risk the chance that they might be rejected or ridiculed.

The Voice says, "What if he laughed at you? That would be awful." "What if she doesn't like you and thinks you're stupid?" Give yourself permission to risk making a positive assertion *even if* you might be rejected.

Positive assertions can range from "Thank you" to "I love you." Try some simple ones first. "I like your dress." "You're new haircut is rad." "I'm glad you're going on the trip, too." "Thanks for the help." "I didn't know you could sing so well. You're good." "I like you." "It was fun talking to you." "I thought your report was interesting." "You're a good friend."

If it's difficult to say positive things to people close to you, begin with people who aren't important to you. Tell a woman in a store that you like her blouse. Tell the secretary at school that she looks especially nice on a day when she does. Say thank you to the cafeteria cashier. Tell the clerk at the store that her hair looks nice. Tell the clerk at the convenience store that you appreciate the good service. After you've practiced for a while you'll find that it gets easier, and then it's time to go on to the harder things. Tell your dad that you appreciate the time he spends with you. Tell your parents that you love them. Tell your best friend that you enjoy spending time with him/her. Tell someone you care about that s/he's important to you. Tell your mom that you appreciate her being there for you. Let yourself feel good by expressing your positive feelings for them.

Expressing Negative Feelings

Instead of looking forward to lunch, Kay Kind dreaded it because of the way she felt about Greta Grumper. By not expressing her feelings to Greta, Kay was failing to treat herself with dignity and respect. She was denying herself the right to be treated with dignity and respect by Greta, and she was carrying around a heavy load of negative feelings that made her feel angry when she was around Greta. Kay was doing what is commonly called "gunnysacking." When Greta said something that bothered Kay, she would think, "I'm not going to make a big deal out of that," and throw it into her gunnysack. However, Kay was holding so much in her gunnysack that she wasn't able to carry it around much longer. She felt she had to avoid Greta because no more could fit into the gunnysack. Although Kay didn't know it, she was afraid she would empty everything out of the sack all over Greta.

Holding negative feelings inside can cause you to want to avoid the people or situations that are producing the feelings if you're like Kay and don't like to show your anger. Many people load up their sack and when they can't hold it any longer, they dump it out, and their anger gets all over anyone in the fall-out zone. Such aggressive behavior hurts both the giver and the receiver. Whether you passively hold on to your anger and then avoid situations and people, or aggressively explode when your sack is full, you need an appropriate way to express your negative feelings. You need a method for keeping your gunnysack empty.

The best time to deal with negative feelings is the very first time you feel uncomfortable. When you're just a little annoyed, you can use an "I" message to give a low-level negative message. If you don't allow your resentments to build, you can deal with them in a calm way. Always remember that *anger should be expressed intentionally in small doses.* When you let your gunnysack fill up, you tend to express your anger unintentionally in a very large dose!

Some people think it's stupid to say anything about a small issue. They think they must have a big issue to be angry about before they say anything. They think they have to have a "good" reason to be mad. You don't have to wait until you think other people think you have a reason to be angry. When Kay first felt irritated was the time to say, "I feel like I'm being told that I'm not doing this right. I'm okay with the way things are going."

You get lots of "muscle power" with "I" messages. When you gunnysack, other people usually don't know that your sack is getting full. They don't even realize that anything they've said or done went into your sack, since you haven't told them. Quite often you come out with guns blazing when all you need is a flyswatter, and the other person is astounded. "I" messages allow you to start with the flyswatter and work up to your big guns. If Greta continues with her helpful suggestions after Kay tells her that she's okay with the way things are going, Kay can add a little muscle. "Greta, I'm okay with the way things are going, and I would rather not have suggestions on what to do." If Greta keeps on, Kay can use a firmer voice and say, "I don't want any suggestions about what I should do to 'get' Greg." If a higher-level muscle is needed, Kay can take Greta aside and say, "Greta, I've tried to be really clear with you that I don't want your suggestions on dealing with Greg. I'm getting angry, and I don't want to hear any more about it."

Each time Kay talked to Greta, she added a little power to her "I" message.

1. "I feel like I'm being told that I'm not doing this right. I'm okay with the way things are going."
2. "Greta, I'm okay with the way things are going, and I would rather not have suggestions on what to do."
3. "I don't want any suggestions about what I should do to 'get' Greg."

4. Taking Greta aside, "Greta, I've tried to be really clear with you that I don't want your suggestions on dealing with Greg. I'm getting angry, and I don't want to hear any more about it."

There may be times when you need to go to a higher level of muscle that involves an authority figure. Mark Merit works in a sporting goods store and has a coworker, Gordon Giddy, who always takes extra long breaks and doesn't relieve Mark on time for his break.

1. "Gordon, I'd appreciate it if you'd relieve me on time for my break. When you're late, I lose that time because I want to relieve Greg on time."
2. "I feel irritated when I'm not relieved on time."
3. "Gordon, this is the third day in a row that you haven't relieved me on time. I'm going to have to report it to Mr. Athleet if you're late again."
4. "Mr. Athleet, I'd appreciate your help in seeing that I'm relieved on time for my break."

Most times you'll be able to express your negative feelings with a low level of muscle. Try these low-level "I" messages to express your negative feelings.

- "I'm annoyed that my book wasn't returned on time."
- "I feel insulted by remarks like that."
- "I don't like my things taken without my permission."
- "I feel taken advantage of when I drive and no one helps pay for the gas."
- "I feel angry when I'm ignored."
- "I don't want help right now."

It may be difficult for you to determine when you need to address an issue. If you're a gunnysacker you won't be sure when it's appropriate to say something. Take a cue from the phrases you use to fill your gunnysack. "It's no big deal." "He was only kidding." "She really didn't mean it." "It doesn't matter." "It's not that bad." "You shouldn't let it bother you." "You're just being sensitive."

To keep your gunnysack empty, it's important to express your feeling when small things happen. It *is* that bad if you toss it into your gunnysack. It really *does* matter if it goes into the sack. You aren't just being sensitive if it hurts enough to go into the sack. You haven't been treated with dignity and respect if you're explaining it away with "She didn't really mean it." Those little bits of unfinished business will become big when they're all in your gunnysack together. A low-level assertive "I" message will take care of things quickly, and most of the time stating your feelings is enough to make you feel comfortable and okay with yourself whether or not the other person responds or takes action. Taking care of yourself is all that's required for your self-esteem.

Expressing Wants and Needs

It would certainly be wonderful if others could guess your wants and needs, but that just doesn't happen. Jenni knew that Phyllis knew that she wanted her video back. Jenni didn't want to ask Phyllis for the video because it's uncomfortable to tell someone that you want something, even if it's something that belongs to you. Because Phyllis didn't bring the video back in a reasonable time, Jenni felt taken advantage of and angry. Allan Apt was feeling frustrated and disappointed when Jenni didn't bring up the subject of chemistry. He needed help, but he didn't want to ask for it. He was hoping Jenni would guess that he needed to talk about the chemistry assignment.

Your wants and needs can be expressed very satisfactorily with "I" messages. A phone call to Phyllis will take care of Jenni. "Phyllis, I'd like to have my Depeche Mode video. I'll meet you at your locker before first period tomorrow to pick it up." Jenni doesn't make a big deal about it, but she does make sure that she sets the time and place for picking it up. Allan's needs could be met with a simple "I" message, too. "I had a hard time following the chemistry lecture today. I could sure use some help with the assignment." Jenni can offer to help or tell Allan that she has so much to do she can't help him tonight. No big deal. If Jenni can't help him tonight, he's no worse off than if he hadn't said anything.

When you need some special understanding from a friend, you can state your needs and get out of the "Guess What I'm Feeling Game." The questions and answers usually go like this: "Is something wrong?" "No. I'm okay." "You don't look okay. Tell me what's wrong." It's like the little kids' game of "Yes You Did, No I Didn't." Express your needs. "I'm feeling down today. I could sure use a friend to listen." Sometimes you may only need someone to be with you. "I need a friend just to be with me for a little while."

Stating wants and needs can be very difficult for some people, and they tend to say other things instead. "It's getting late," probably means "I want to go home." "Is the heater on?" can be translated to "I'm cold." When you call home and tell your mother. "You gotta be here by 5:30," she may tell you that she doesn't "gotta be" anywhere. If instead you say, "I need to be at the rehearsal by 6 o'clock," she'll probably tell you that she'll pick you up at 5:30. "I" messages stating needs get considerate, respectful attention most of the time. Try these "I" messages for stating wants and needs.

- "I need a ride."
- "I would like my book returned."
- "I need a little time alone."
- "I want to go home now."
- "I need to know you better before I go out with you."
- "I want to be on time for the movie."
- "I need to know when you're supposed to be in tonight."

Stating your wants and needs saves all the guessing and hoping that goes on when you aren't direct. You save yourself disappointment and frustration, and you save others the confusion of guessing and being wrong. Asking for what you want and need gives you power and control over your own life. You can feel good about taking care of yourself.

Setting Limits

Saying yes when she wanted to say no was Peggy Pleezer's big problem. She always felt trapped into doing things and then felt resentful toward the people she thought had trapped her. Peggy always had the option to say no, but she didn't take it. She was afraid people wouldn't like her or would be mad at her if she said no. What other people thought was very important to Peggy, and what *she* thought was lost in her efforts to please others. She allowed others to infringe on her rights, and they didn't know it because Peggy never told them. Her inability to set limits caused her to feel bad about herself.

When people ask you to do things you don't want to do, you may feel that you have to give them a good reason in order to refuse. If you're asked to do something you want to do and you say yes, does anyone ask you why? If you're not obligated to give a reason for your yes, why should you be obligated to give a reason for no? Sometimes you may just not want to do something. That's okay. When Debi asked Peggy to fill in at the Little League hot dog stand, there was an assertive way for Peggy to handle it.

Debi: Peggy, I have to go to the dentist today and it's my turn to sell hot dogs at Davy's game. Could you be a real friend and fill in for me?

Peggy: Sorry, Debi, not today.

Debi: Oh, I really need to find somebody. Couldn't you do it just this once?

Peggy: Not today, Debi.

Debi: I'll do you a favor when you need it.

Peggy: Not today.

Debi: What's so important that you can't do it today?

Peggy: Sorry, Debi, not today.

Debi: Well, I don't know what I'll do.

Peggy: I hope you find someone. Bye, Debi.

Saying no to Debi was done in a way that treated both girls with dignity and respect. Rather than get into finding excuses for not selling hot dogs, Peggy said no very firmly and politely. She did nothing to hurt Debi's feelings and took care of her own needs very appropriately.. To stay out of arguing and making excuses, Peggy used the "broken record" technique. She said, "Not today," and offered nothing else. Sometimes people will insist on knowing why or will try to make you feel guilty for not doing what they want you to do. Stick with your broken record and don't try to reason with them. Even if they get angry, it's okay for you to say no. You have every right to refuse to do something you don't want to do. If you do something that you really don't want to do, you'll feel resentful and take it out on the person you resent or on yourself. Doing what you don't want to do will be much worse for you in the long run than if you hold to your no and let others think what they will. Remember, what they think is none of your business.

Phyllis: This is a neat video, Jenni. Can I borrow it?
Jenni: I don't want to lend that video, Phyllis.
Phyllis: I'll take care of it.
Jenni: I don't want to lend that video.
Phyllis: Why not?
Jenni: I don't want to lend that video.
Phyllis: I'll bring it back tomorrow.
Jenni: I don't want to lend that video.
Phyllis: All right.

If Jenni gets into explaining why she's doesn't want to lend the video, it will end in an argument with Phyllis feeling hurt and Jenni feeling guilty, or Jenni will give in because she can't come up with a "good enough" reason. The "broken record" saves all that wear and tear.

Asking you to do favors is only one way that people cross your personal boundaries and need to be limited. You may not realize how often your boundaries are crossed because you may not be aware that you have boundaries. Some of the ways in which others do not respect your boundaries are dropping in to see you without calling first; telephoning at inconvenient times; borrowing things and not returning them; never having money with them so you pay; asking for rides; expecting you to cover for them when they lie; wanting you to do what you don't want to do.

To deal with people who cross your boundaries, "I" messages work very well.

- "That's my favorite sweater, Phyllis, and I don't want to lend it."
- "I don't have money for both of us tonight."
- "I don't have time to visit right now. Please call before you come over."
- "It's dinner time and I can't talk right now. If you call between 8 and 9 I can talk to you then."

You may often feel pressure from others to do what they want you to do, go where they want you to go, or be the way they want you to be. You always have the right to say no and to do what is comfortable for you. When you feel uncomfortable, listen to your Inner Being and treat it with respect. Saying no with dignity and respect does not infringe on the rights of others; it allows you to protect your rights and treat yourself with dignity and respect.

Coping with Criticism Assertively

Criticism hurts so much because you want approval from others, and criticism lets you know that you're not approved of one hundred percent. It tells you that you're not perfect and insinuates that you're wrong and the other person is right. It says that you're doing something wrong and there's a better way to do it. It attacks your Inner Being and gives the Voice ammunition for further attacks. Criticism can cause you to feel so uncomfortable that you go against your Inner Being in order to satisfy the critical judgments of other people.

There are many kinds of criticism. Some can be positive and helpful when given in a supportive way by people who are truly motivated to help you. The most usual criticism is negative, however, and does nothing but nag and complain about your real or imagined failings. Some people use criticism to put you down so they'll look good or make you wrong so they'll be right. Whenever there's a disagreement, it seems that people feel it's necessary for one to be wrong and one to be right. That's not true. You can be different without being wrong. You just don't see things the same way. It's okay to be different. No one has to be right. It's okay to disagree. It's okay to think differently.

The most common feelings triggered by criticism are guilt, fear, and anxiety. When you allow someone to make you wrong, you feel guilty. The fear and anxiety come when you think that others don't like and approve of you. Those feelings can come through criticism that is true, untrue, partly true, or hurtful and unjustified. When coping with criticism, the goal is not winning or getting even or being right. The goal is to protect your feelings and your rights without infringing on the rights of others, treating them with dignity and respect while maintaining your own dignity and self-respect.

The common thing about all negative criticism is that you don't want it. You've learned some ways to deal with the critical Voice, and now you need some ways to deal with other people in your life who criticize you.

Agreeing with Criticism

If negative criticism is justified, it's important to acknowledge and accept it rather than to be defensive about it. When you agree with the critic, the criticism will usually stop immediately. When your mother says, "This room is a filthy mess," and it is, it's time to say, "You're right, it's pretty bad." It puts an end to the attack on you without defending and arguing, and it says that you're okay even though the criticism may be correct.

Mrs. Dapper: You're so careless with your things. I found this sweater on the back steps.
Debi: You're right. I was careless with that sweater. Thanks for bringing it in.

Allan: You're always late. We're supposed to be at Connie's now.
Steve: You're right. I'm running late tonight.

Trisha: When are you going to wash your car? You can hardly see the license plate.
Bruce: You're right, it's really dirty. First weekend I have off I'll wash it.

Mrs. Apt: It's nine-thirty. You said you'd be home by nine.
Allan: You're right, Mom, I'm late. I didn't plan on stopping at Kevin's when I took him home. I should have called you from there. Sorry.

Mr. Alert: This paper looks as if you wrote it while you were eating and dripped all over it. What a mess!
Dan: You're right, it is a mess. I need to work on being neater.

When you agree with criticism that's justified, you defuse the critics. They need resistance to keep them rolling.

They can't keep up the bombardment if you don't give them any ammunition. When you agree with them, you take away the target. They'll usually stop because they have the satisfaction of being right and no longer have to continue trying to convince you of how bad or how wrong you are.

Agreeing is used only when the criticism is true. If you agree with criticism that's untrue, you've gone against your Inner Being and will affect your own self-esteem. When criticism is untrue, the most effective way to deal with it is through "fogging."

Fogging

The originator of the term "fogging" is Manuel Smith, who wrote *When I Say No I Feel Guilty*. Fogging is a way of neither agreeing nor disagreeing. It's like walking through a fog. The fog is there, can be seen, but it doesn't change you nor can you change it. You walk through it unharmed. You never attack or defend, agree or disagree. You merely fog away the criticism.

Mr. Zero: If you'd study for the tests, your grades would be better.

Dan: You may be right. Mr. Zero.

Phyllis: You're just being selfish not to lend the video.

Jenni: It may seem that way to you, Phyllis.

Brad: You don't know how to have a good time.

Allan: It probably seems that way to you.

Ms. Fauna: You could have an A if you tried.

Felicia: That's probably true.

Art: You're so slow. We'll never make the movie on time.

Steve: I guess I seem slow to you.

The phrases that create the fog are: "You *may* be right...." "It *probably seems* so...." "That's *probably* true...." "It *may seem* so to you...." "I *guess it seems*...." When Felicia says it's probably true that she could get an A if she tried, she's also saying that it may not be true. "I guess I seem slow to you" doesn't agree or disagree. Steve's okay with his speed and it seems fine to him. "It may seem so to you" doesn't necessarily mean that it seems so to me. *May, seem,* and *probably* are all words that say nothing in particular. "You may be right" could mean that you may be wrong. When you fog, you're not making anyone right or anyone wrong. You can choose to change or not to change. You maintain your dignity and respect without the need for defending or attacking. You can feel good about yourself and the way you handled the situation.

Disagreeing with Criticism

When criticism is unjust or untrue, it's appropriate to disagree with the person giving the criticism. You don't want people to keep treating you unfairly or to continue seeing you in a way that is distorted and untrue.

Phyllis: You're really getting selfish lately, Jenni.

Jenni: I'm not selfish, Phyllis. I just don't want to lend my favorite videos.

When Phyllis puts on the negative label of "selfish," Jenni refuses to take it on and feel guilty. She has every right to refuse to lend her property to Phyllis without justifying it.

> Ms. Fauna: If you'd just study harder, your test grades would improve, Missie.
>
> Missie: Ms. Fauna, I study as hard as I can for every test. Zoology is very difficult for me, and I'm working hard to do my very best.

It was important for Missie that Ms. Fauna know she had studied hard and was making every effort to do her best work. People who put too high expectations on Missie are being unfair and need to be aware of how hard she is working. Whenever you've been unfairly criticized, it is important to *you* to disagree with dignity.

Disagreeing in Part

There are times when you are criticized and part of the criticism is true. In those cases you agree with the part that's true and disagree with the part that isn't.

> Allan: You're always late. Why can't you be ready on time?
>
> Steve: You're right, I was late tonight, but this is the first time I've been late since you mentioned it to me over a month ago.

> Mom: Why can't you do anything right? This cord is to be wrapped around the handle so it doesn't get all tangled in the drawer.
>
> Felicia: I wasn't careful this time with the cord, but

> I don't always do things wrong. I do a good
> job most of the time.

Mr. Zero: You're always late. I'm going to have to
start giving detention for tardiness.

Larry: I've been late twice this week because I've
been helping Ms. Fauna set up a zoology
display. I can get a pass from her if you
want me to. This is the first time I've been
late for your class all year.

There was some truth to each of the complaints, but part
of the criticism was not true. Larry and Steve weren't
always late, and Felicia did do some things right. In each
case, they agreed with the part of the criticism that was
correct and disagreed with what was untrue. Whenever
you disagree with criticism, it's important to pay attention
to your tone of voice so you don't sound sharp or defensive.
In order to treat yourself with dignity and respect, you
must treat others in a dignified, respectful way.

Delaying

Coming up with exactly the right thing to say in every
instance would be wonderful if it were humanly possible.
Since it isn't, you may be uncertain or confused sometimes
and need some time to think about it. Be assertive and say,
"I'm not sure how I feel about that. I'd like to think about it
and talk about it later." Pamela Butler in her book *Self-
Assertion for Women* calls that "delaying." If you feel confused, say, "I feel confused about that and need some time
to think about it," or "I'd like to think about that and talk
about it later."

When you use delaying, the important thing is to make sure that you do bring it up later. A simple way to do that is to say, "I've thought about..., and I agree with...," or, "I've thought about..., and I disagree with..." There is nothing wrong with taking time to sort out your feelings and get in touch with your Inner Being. When you take that extra time, you allow yourself to decide on an appropriate way to respond rather than simply reacting to the moment.

There may be times when you're so confused or stunned that you can't think of anything to say; you can't remember how to delay. You may think that you've lost out completely. Not so. You can always bring up what's bothering you. It may be an hour, a day, a week, a month, or a year since it happened, but if it's bothering you, you can bring it up. A simple way to open it up is to say, "I have something that's bothering me, and I need to share it with you." Your Voice will try to talk you out of it by saying that you're being dumb or it's too late. The Voice always lies. If something's eating at you, it's unfinished business and needs to be taken care of. You can be honest when you want to talk about it. "There's something I need to talk about. I feel kind of dumb bringing it up, but it's been bothering me and I need to talk about it." It's never too late to be assertive and take care of yourself.

Self-assertion and Self-esteem

Knowing your feelings is the basis for knowing who you are. Expressing your feelings is how you let others know who you are. Standing up for what you believe is nothing more than listening to your Inner Being who speaks to you through your feelings, trusting those feelings, and not allowing others or your Voice to keep you from expressing those feelings through your words or behavior. The heart of self-assertion is trusting your feelings. Criticism from others and your Voice has made you distrustful of your own feelings. It's time to say yes to yourself.

When others disagree with you, your tendency is to go along with the group. Keep in mind that when you disagree with people, no one has to be wrong. You can just disagree. What you think and feel, your opinion, is as valid as anyone else's, and for you it's more valid. Your feelings, wants, and needs are important, and the Voice is not your friend. It wants to talk you into believing that what you think is wrong. Listen to your Inner Being. Pay attention to those feelings and stand up for them. By standing up for your beliefs, you won't go along with behavior that's not good for you. You'll be true to your Inner Being and feel good about yourself.

Passive and aggressive behavior tear down your self-esteem. When you're passive and allow others to infringe on your rights and take advantage of you, you feel bad about yourself. You know you've let yourself down, and you resent the people whom you've allowed to treat you disrespectfully. Your lack of respect for yourself encourages others to be inconsiderate and disrespectful toward you. When you're aggressive you protect your rights at all costs, disregarding the rights of others. You may feel powerful, strong, and self-righteous, but you also feel lonely because so many people don't want to be around you and guilty because you know you've treated people shabbily. You're probably a little afraid that others will find out that under that rough and tough shell you're afraid of being hurt yourself. Losing the positive regard of others because of passive or aggressive behavior is not the highest price you pay. The greatest loss is the loss of personal dignity and self-respect that causes loss of self-esteem.

Being assertive builds self-esteem because you are true to yourself and treat yourself and others with dignity and respect. Don't be concerned whether others treat you with dignity and respect. RESPECT FOR YOURSELF MUST COME BEFORE OTHERS CAN RESPECT YOU. Assertiveness gives you the means for treating yourself with dignity and respect because how *you* feel about *you* is what's important. By being assertive you acknowledge your Inner Being and express your feelings in an appropriate way. You don't put anyone down. You don't get into power struggles that make someone a loser. You may not always get your way or achieve your goals, but you'll feel that you've handled yourself in a way that is acceptable and positive for you. You'll feel good that you've been direct and open and honest. As you become more and more assertive, your self-confidence will grow as will your self-respect. As your self-respect grows, you'll notice that you're treated more respectfully by others and that somewhere along the way that elusive intangible called self-esteem became yours.

CHAPTER 10

Essentials of Self-esteem

The church youth group had been meeting with Frank Friendly for almost three months, and Stephanie Stable was excited about tonight's meeting. After each meeting Stephanie had gone home and shared with her mother. She was amazed at how much closer she felt to her mother since she'd been doing that. When Stephanie shared, her mother, Stella, would share in return, and Stephanie had found out so much about her mother that she hadn't known. Her mother was a real person to her now, not just her mother, and Stephanie felt that she was treated on a more equal basis by her mother.

When Stephanie and Stella had talked about how being assertive helps to build self-esteem. Stella shared some ideas she'd found in Nathaniel Branden's book *Honoring the Self*. Stephanie wanted to hear the reactions and ideas of the group to five things Branden said were required for self-esteem. When she showed Frank the list, he agreed that it would be a good basis for the group's discussion. Frank wrote the following list on the board:

Self-esteem requires:
1. Independent thinking
2. Integrity
3. Self-responsibility
4. Self-acceptance
5. Internalizing

As soon as Frank opened the discussion, Felicia began to give her feelings and ideas about independent thinking. She told the group how Connie Jeanial had stood up for what she believed and hadn't been involved in TPing houses with the crowd. "I remember thinking how brave Connie was to be the only one not to go along with the gang. I'd have joined in and wouldn't have given it a second thought at the time. Connie really made me think about my behavior, and coming to group has made me aware that I need to think for myself and not just go along with other people."

The next to speak was Steve Strain. "Thinking independently is really hard for me. I used to let what other people think rule me. I didn't trust myself or my feelings at all. Since I've been coming to group, I realize that what other people think is none of my business, but it's been really hard for me to believe that strongly enough not to be influenced by what other people think. I feel real insecure, and I'm afraid people won't like me if I don't agree with them. I'm getting better about thinking for myself though. The other day I was down at the playground with my little brother, and after I pushed his swing for him, I decided to swing myself. Rudy Goash came by and started bugging me about falling off and getting hurt. For the first time I didn't let it bother me. I said, 'That's a possibility,' and kept right on swinging. I felt real anxious and afraid that he'd make a big deal out of it, but he just laughed and walked away. That may not seem like much to anybody, but it was really big for me. I think it's okay for me to swing if I want to, and I'm going to do it!'"

After the group stopped cheering for Steve, several others shared how thinking independently was really scary for them at first. Everyone agreed that the first time they'd stood up for their ideas, feelings, or beliefs was the hardest. Once they'd hung in through the uncertainty and insecurity, it was less difficult the next time, and as they became more assertive, standing by their beliefs became easier. No one was feeling like a pro, but they were doing better.

Trisha Trendy confessed that she was still trying to figure out what she really thought about things. She'd gone along with things for so long that she didn't even know what she liked most of the time. It was just the other day that she looked at herself in a full-length mirror and decided that she didn't care how "in" high-top shoes were, she really thought they looked ugly. "I'd been wearing them for months because *everybody* who was *anybody* was wearing them. I dropped them in the barrel for the church Clothes Closet on the way here tonight, and I feel good."

When everyone who wanted to had shared, they went on to the second thing on the list, integrity. Frank wanted to be sure they were all talking about the same thing, so he asked the group to tell what they thought integrity was. "It's standing up for what you believe," was one offering. "How do you do that?" was Frank's next question. "By not being afraid to tell people." "By doing what you believe is right even if no one else agrees with you." "By doing what you believe is right even when you don't want to."

As the discussion of integrity went on, the group began to offer experiences and examples. "The other day Tracy Carbon wanted to copy my history homework," began Art Affable, "and I really didn't want to let him have it, but I did. I felt really bad about myself, like I had let myself down. I think that was an example of when you don't have integrity. I know now that I don't want to do that again. It'll be really hard to say no, but I have to if I want to feel good about myself."

"I know what you mean," interjected Polly Perfect. "If I do something I don't think is right or don't do something I know to do, I feel really bad about myself. This may seem silly to you, but as Steve was talking I remembered an incident that happened about a month ago. I was walking by the playground on my way home and heard someone I won't name teasing a little boy. The little kid was crying and this person was laughing at him. I wanted to tell him to leave the kid alone, and I wanted to comfort the little boy. I didn't say a word. I just walked on minding my own business. I've felt bad ever since. There was somebody I knew being so cruel, and I just walked on by. I was afraid he'd think I was messing in his business and be mad at me. Now I realize that I needed to tell him how cruel I thought he was. I think I showed a lack of integrity when I didn't do that, and my self-esteem was really affected."

"I know how you feel," chimed in Jenni Jentry. "I think I know what it feels like when integrity is missing. It's like I believe something and feel that it's right, but when it comes time to *do* something about it I just can't seem to do it. I guess my Voice takes over and tells me that everybody will think I'm stupid or it's none of my business or nobody's going to listen to me anyway. But when I just let it go, I feel really bad. Like Art said, I feel like I let myself down."

"So what is integrity, then?" repeated Frank. After a

little more discussion, Harry Hardy said, "I think it means you act the way you believe and feel, and I think it means you're honest even when nobody's looking. I was reading a magazine the other day, and it told how a junior high girl in a national spelling bee misspelled a word and the judges didn't hear the mistake. She told them that she had spelled it wrong. I think that's what integrity is about."

"Let me summarize," said Frank. "It seems to me you're saying that integrity involves doing what you believe is right even when it's scary; it means standing up for what you believe in even if you're the only one; it's being honest when nobody's looking—I like that, Harry; it says it very well—and it means that you behave according to your convictions and beliefs."

"And being assertive helps us do that," added Stephanie Stable. "That's where that fits in. It gives us a way to express ourselves with dignity and respect. I'm glad you worked on that with us, Frank, because now I feel I have a way to maintain my integrity without messing with anybody else's."

Frank chuckled and thanked Stephanie for stating it so well and moved on to the third item on the list, self-responsibility. There was a short silence and Peggy Pleezer began to talk. "This one is really hard for me. I've always thought that I'm a real responsible person, and people have told me how responsible I am since I was a little kid. I hate to say this, but I'm not very *self*-responsible at all. I take responsibility for everybody else. I feel responsible for my sister's messes and clean up after her all the time. Teachers ask me to help them because I'm so dependable and responsible. I'll do jobs for everybody else because I can't say no. All the time I'm being responsible for everybody else, I'm really taking care of myself. I haven't told people how I really feel. I'm just beginning to be able to say no. I've been so busy pleasing everybody else, I'm not sure that I know what I really like and what I really want. For being such a responsible person, I haven't done such a hot job being responsible for myself."

"Woooo, Peggy. I never thought of it that way. I always thought you were super responsible." The look of surprise on Dan Dawdle's face disappeared as he began to talk. "When I think of self-responsibility, I think of being responsible about doing what I'm supposed to do, and I'm not too good at that. I let my homework go to the very last minute, and my mother is always nagging me about doing my chores around the house. My room would be a toxic waste site if my mother didn't make me sort through the garbage and junk every once in a while. I wait for somebody else to come up with an idea for something to do on the weekend so I don't have to bother figuring out what I want to do. I really haven't been very responsible for myself. Then my Voice beats on me and I feel bad about myself. I'm beginning to see how my irresponsibility works against me. I'm just hurting myself when I'm not responsible for myself. That doesn't feel good to say, but I know it's true. I guess if I'm going to have any integrity, I'm going to have to look at self-responsibility, too."

Frank nodded and said, "That's very perceptive of you, Dan. There is definitely a connection between self-responsibility and integrity. That's what you were saying too, Peggy. When you don't know your own beliefs and feelings, you certainly can't stand up for them. You're really pretty helpless."

"You know, I think going along with the gang is a way of not being responsible for yourself," Felicia remarked thoughtfully. "I just can't get Connie out of my mind. She was taking full responsibility for what she believed. When you just go along, you're not being responsible. You're giving other people power over you. You're letting them decide what you believe, think, or feel at that moment. I haven't been very responsible for myself in a lot of ways, and my mother has always praised me for being responsible. What she means by responsible is doing what she tells me to do when she tells me to do it. I take responsibility for my homework, and I help around the house and get home on time and stuff like that. But I just do things because I'm *supposed* to. I don't think about it. Since we've been talking about self-esteem and assertiveness and everything, I'm beginning to look at what *I* think and what *I* believe. I'm not very assertive yet because I'm not sure *what* to be assertive about! I think it all comes down to my needing to be responsible for my beliefs and feelings, but first I have to find out what they are. Group has helped a lot, but I have a long way to go."

"Yeah, that's the way I feel," said Art Affable. "I go along with the guys, and then I end up being mad because of stuff that happens. I got talked into going to a party at somebody's house I didn't even know. People just went there to get drunk and stoned. I didn't want to be there, but I hung around because I was with some guys. That didn't show much self-responsibility, but I thought I was being real responsible because I was driving and didn't drink. I needed to get myself out of there or, better yet, not to have gone at all. That's what self-responsibility is all about. Instead, I blamed everybody else because I didn't have a good time. I always blame everybody else for messing things up for me, but I'm the one who isn't responsible for myself. I can see that now."

"You're bringing out some really good points," Frank said, "and you're seeing some important relationships. I'm impressed with how deeply you're thinking and how many risks you're taking with your sharing. You've built a lot of trust in the group and it shows."

"You know, Frank, I've been thinking about how much I talk about wanting to be responsible for myself, but when I have the responsibility, I don't always want to keep it." This time it was Larry Leery. "I have a job and I'm saving for a car, but I keep part of what I earn for spending money. I think that's pretty responsible, but when I blow all my money I know my folks will lend me some until pay day. Sometimes if it's just a couple of bucks, my dad will tell me not to bother when I go to pay him back. If I really were self-responsible, I'd be more careful with my money or I'd just go without until pay day. Now, this is just an example, it doesn't mean that I'm going to quit borrowing from my dad!"

Still laughing, Steve said, "Don't give my parents any ideas. It's hard enough to borrow now. I know what you're saying, though. I really love animals and like to have lots of pets. When I first started collecting what my mother calls my zoo, I agreed that I'd take care of my animals. That was no big deal, I thought, because it wasn't much trouble to feed little hamsters and goldfish. What I forgot was that cages and bowls have to be cleaned. I didn't want that responsibility, and I'd ignore it until my mother would have fits about the smell. So, in a way, she took over the responsibility for seeing that cages and bowls were cleaned because she'd remind me and remind me until I did it. Actually, I let it go until she got mad enough that I knew I'd better do it. I'm doing better with that now because I know how bad it is for the animals, but it took me a while to keep that responsibility myself."

"That's quite an insight, Steve," Frank commented.

"Let's see if I can summarize this. Self-responsibility means more than just being a responsible person who does chores and homework and all the things you're "supposed" to do. Self-responsibility is taking responsibility for your beliefs and feelings and expressing them. It means taking responsibility for your own thinking and not just going along with the gang. It's part of your integrity because you take responsibility and stand up for your beliefs. Some of you feel that you take lots of responsibility for others but don't do a very good job of knowing your own wants and needs and taking care of them. Others of you feel that you want responsibility until you get it, and like Steve and Larry, you wait for others to pick up your slack. There aren't many adults who would make those connections, gang. That's quite a job of looking at yourselves. With that to build on, what do you understand about self-acceptance?"

"That's the hardest one for me," said Polly Perfect. Heads nodded all around the group, and Polly went on. "There are so many things I don't like about myself that it's really hard to accept myself."

"Do you think you have to like everything about yourself before you can accept yourself?" asked Frank.

"Well, don't you?"

"Of course not. Accepting yourself and approving of everything about yourself are two different things. In fact, an important part of acceptance is accepting the things you disapprove of in yourself. Those are the things you want to change. Peggy sees that she's responsible for everyone but herself. She doesn't like that, and she's working on changing it. She's only been able to see the need to change since she's accepted that quality that she doesn't approve of in herself. Some people have the idea that if we accept something in ourselves we'll never change it. That isn't true at all. Admitting that it's there and we don't like it is the first step toward change.

"Some things can't be changed. If you don't like your big feet, even if you accept them you can't change them. As long as you resist them, you'll be uncomfortable and unhappy. Accept the fact of your big feet and let it go at that. It's kind of like ending the war and learning to live with your former enemies."

"That's easy to say, Frank, but when you have braces on your teeth that make your mouth look ugly whether it's open or closed and they hurt besides, it's pretty hard to make friends." Several heads nodded in agreement with Harry Hardy. "I'd like to say that it's okay to have braces," continued Harry, "but I don't think it's okay."

"Can you say, 'I don't like it but that's the way it is'?" Heads nodded and Frank went on. "That's a beginning move toward acceptance. Will feeling bad about it change it?" A chorus of no's followed. "Will being angry make them go away?" More no's. "Can you hate them and yet tell your Voice that you're not going to listen to its anger making remarks that only make things worse?" That was a little harder for the braces wearers. "Can you tell the Voice that it's worth the hassle now because of the payoff later?"

"I'm not sure I believe that right this minute. They look *so* ugly," moaned Jenni.

"Jenni, you're so cute, your braces don't make you look ugly!" Everyone looked at Larry, who blushed and said, "Well, I just meant I don't think braces make people look ugly."

"I don't either," declared Stephanie. "You know what I think? We each pick out something that we don't like about ourselves and then blow it up all out of proportion and hate it. The Voice makes us do that to keep us from accepting ourselves. I don't like my nose, but it's the only nose I have right now. Later on, if I want to have it changed, I can, but right now it doesn't do me any good to let hating it make me hate myself. I never thought of that before, Frank, I see what you mean now."

"I hate it because I'm so uncoordinated and look so clumsy in P.E. I guess if I would accept that, maybe I could just say, 'Oh, well, I'm a good clarinet player,' and let it go at that." Felicia shrugged her shoulders and looked questioningly at Frank.

"That's the idea, Felicia. When you do that, you're accepting the good stuff about yourself, too. Don't forget how important that is," Frank reminded them.

"So self-acceptance means I accept that there are some things I like about myself and some things I don't like." Dan Dawdle looked thoughtful and spoke slowly. "Some of the things I don't like I can't do anything about—like my height or the fact that I have to wear glasses. Some things I don't like I can do something about—like being more responsible for myself. The important thing is that I accept myself just the way I am and then do the best I can with what I've got."

"And the things I like about myself I can give myself credit for and try to make even better! Right, Frank?"

"You got it, Polly! It's a thing of saying, 'Here I am, warts and all.' It's being the best 'me' you can be right now. After you accept who and what you are, you can go for a change, and sometimes the only change you can make is how *you* look at things—such as your attitude about your braces. Sometimes you can make some significant changes because of insights into your behavior. You're talking big change, Felicia, when you talk about the independent thinking and the integrity of not going along with the crowd. Can you see how you've accepted your old way of thinking, decided you didn't like it, and are now looking at a new way? That's really big stuff, and you haven't been feeling down on yourself for not thinking about it sooner. That's real acceptance." Frank looked around the group and asked for any other comments. When there were none he brought the discussion to the final thing on the list, internalizing.

After a short silence. Polly began to speak. "I guess it makes sense that self-esteem would come from within you. If it's *my* self-esteem, it must come from inside *me*, but I know that I've been trying to get things outside myself to make me feel good."

"What things?" Frank asked, quietly.

Everyone was listening intently and waiting expectantly for Polly's answer. "Well, I thought if I got good grades, I'd feel good because my parents would be happy. And I thought if I could dress the way Trisha does, I'd feel good about myself because I looked good. I thought if only I were popular, I'd feel good about myself because everybody liked me. I thought if I were cuter I'd feel better about myself. I kept looking for somebody else to tell me that I'm okay, but no matter how many people said good things about me, I never felt good enough. Now I can see that it's because *I* didn't accept myself. I wasn't perfect, and the Voice wouldn't let me be okay without being perfect. Since we did our Voice notebook, Frank, I've been telling my Voice that it's okay if I'm not perfect and it's okay if I make a mistake. That's helped me a lot, and I like myself better now. I'm really glad that we talked about this stuff today, because I needed to know that I can accept things that I don't like about myself. One of the biggest things I don't like is that I have such a hard time when I'm not perfect, but I'm working to change that. I accept myself much more now, and I can tell that my self-esteem is going up; and it's going up because I'm telling *myself* that I'm an okay person."

"That's really neat, Polly. I never thought you ever felt that way because that's the way I feel—about wanting everybody else to think I'm okay." Peggy Pleezer was leaning forward enthusiastically. "That's why I always let myself get stuck doing things for everybody else. I want them to like me so I can like me, but what happens is I feel resentful for getting stuck doing so much and I feel mad about agreeing to do it. I used to think that other people made me feel bad, but I felt bad because I didn't say no. You know the assertiveness stuff on setting limits really made me see how I made myself feel bad. So it stands to reason that if I'm responsible for making myself feel bad, I must be responsible for making myself feel good, too."

"I just wish it were as easy to make myself feel good as it is to make myself feel bad," Art said ruefully, and everyone laughed. He went on, "I guess this is one of those self-responsibility things, too. If I want to feel good, I have to take the responsibility to do things and act in ways that make me feel good about myself. I have to stop blaming other people for making me feel bad. When I get down on myself, it's because I don't like what's going on with me right then. So that has to do with self-acceptance. What I can see now is that all four of the other things on the list come from inside. It all has to work together. When all of those things are working for us, or we make them work for us, we're okay because we're taking care of our Inner Being."

"That's very well put, Art. That interrelationship of the five essentials is very important." Frank looked around the group and noticed that Harry looked as though he might be ready to share.

Harry began to speak as Frank nodded. "I think I've been waiting all my life for my father to approve of me, but I've never thought he approved of me enough. I've never thought that I'm good enough in anything for him to accept me a hundred percent. Now I can see that even when he does accept me, I don't think I'm quite good enough. I'm always afraid that I'll mess up next time and not be good enough. I think what I'm getting at is that if *I* don't accept me and think I'm good enough, it doesn't matter if he or anyone else does. It won't be enough until *I* think it's enough."

"That's exactly how I feel, Harry." Missie Meek spoke up for the first time. "No matter how hard I try, my mother can always find something wrong with what I've done. If I bake brownies, she was wishing for chocolate chip cookies. I know she isn't going to give me credit for doing well. I have to start saying I'm okay. Lots of times I do a good job, but I never give myself credit for it. I always think everybody else is better or smarter or faster or whatever. I'm not all that bad, and I need to accept my good points and take care of myself."

"Yes, you do, Missie. Thanks for sharing." Frank looked at the serious faces and asked if there was any feedback or further sharing.

"I want to thank Missie and Harry for sharing what they did," Trisha said as she looked around the group. "That's how I feel, too, sometimes. It seems to me that my sister gets all the attention and approval, and I feel left out a lot. I try to do things so my mom will approve of me, but most of the time she doesn't notice what I do. She picks at me about the things I don't do. I think I can't be okay if she doesn't like everything I do. I know that isn't reasonable, but I feel that way. What can I do about that, Frank?"

"That might be something you have to say you don't like

but accept, and then look inside yourself for *your* approval. When you stop looking for approval from your parents and other people and things outside of yourself, you'll be surprised at how much approval you get. Another thing to consider is practicing in group some nonthreatening, assertive ways to let your folks know how you're feeling. When you get some unjust criticism, you can deal with it assertively. It's important to be assertive with your parents, and you can work it out here in group."

"I like that idea, Frank," Harry said. "I'd be willing to work on that, too," added Missie. "Me, too," chimed in Polly and Trisha together. Heads were nodding all around the group.

"It looks like we have group planned for next time. Thanks, Stephanie, for sharing the list of essentials of self-esteem. You've taught me a lot tonight, group, and I appreciate your honesty and thoughtfulness. I'm looking forward to seeing you next week." As Frank watched the group leave, he noticed that Trisha, Polly, and Peggy were waiting at the door for Missie. He could sense that tonight's sharing had created a bond between Missie and the other girls.

You and Your Self-esteem

In looking at the five essentials of self-esteem, the group discovered that self-esteem happens from the inside out. To be an independent thinker you have to be aware of your feelings and your values, and you must have a willingness to stand up for what you believe. Felicia tended to take on the values of whomever she was around, and Peggy was so "other-focused" that it didn't occur to her that she might have feelings of her own. How could they have self-esteem when they had no real sense of self?

When you develop self-awareness, which is the knowledge of your values and feelings, you're able to make conscious choices that enhance your self-esteem. You're no longer running on automatic pilot without having to fly your own plane. You have full responsibility for taking care of your own self-esteem, and the foundation for doing that is being assertive. Through self-assertion you can express your feelings and beliefs. *No one* can make you feel bad unless you allow it. *No one* can tear down your self-esteem unless you let them. *No one* can give you self-esteem. No one but *you* can build and maintain your self-esteem. You can allow your Voice to add the criticism and fault-finding of others to its arsenal for killing your self-esteem, or you can fight the Voice to keep your self-esteem alive and growing. It truly is up to you.

As the group working with Frank Friendly realized, self-responsibility is tied up in the same package with independent thinking and integrity. Maintaining your integrity, that inner feeling of honesty and honor, can happen only if you take responsibility for your feelings and beliefs and stick with them no matter what anyone else thinks.

There are two distinct parts of you: your values—what you believe to be good and right for you—and your behavior. When your behavior is in sync with your values, you feel good about yourself, and your self-esteem is maintained. When your behavior isn't consistent with your values, you feel bad about yourself, and your self-esteem goes down. Art didn't feel comfortable at the party because the drinking and drug use were against his values. Just by being there, even though he didn't drink or use, he lost some of his self-esteem. He didn't take responsibility for his feelings or beliefs, his sense of integrity was tainted, and, as a result, his self-esteem was affected.

Any time you behave in a way that isn't consistent with

your values, the two parts of you separate. You can feel the pull from inside yourself. In a sense, it's your Inner Being saying "Ouch." If you ignore the warning and continue to behave in ways that are out of sync with your values, the separation grows, and you begin to hurt inside. The way the hurt is transmitted to you is through a loss of self-esteem. For people who continue behaving in self-destructive ways, the separation becomes so great that they lose touch with their Inner Being. Aggressive, angry people who don't treat themselves or others with dignity and respect are examples of people who've lost touch with their Inner Being. No matter what kind of front those people put up, they're actually hurting inside and suffering from extremely low self-esteem.

When you're hurting inside, look at your behavior and see if you acted in a way that affected your integrity. Some ways you maintain integrity are:

- Standing up for what you believe in.
- Taking care of your feelings assertively.
- Dealing with criticism effectively.
- Doing what you believe to be right and good for you.
- Being honest when nobody's looking.
- Thinking independently.
- Taking responsibility for your feelings and behavior.

When you feel that you haven't behaved with integrity, the tendency is to allow your Voice to punish you. Being unhappy with your behavior is part of being human. To maintain your self-esteem in spite of your human failings and imperfections takes talking back to your Voice, which wants to criticize you and tear you down. Your Voice works against self-acceptance. Those times that you don't like your behavior, admit it and tell the Voice that it's something you're working on. Accept all of your behavior as part of you. You don't have to like it or approve of it, just accept it. It's self-acceptance that allows you to change the behavior that hurts you, that tears down your self-esteem.

Your self-esteem can suffer when you don't like something about yourself that you can't change. Harry didn't like his braces, and Stephanie hated her nose. You may think you're too tall, too short, too thin, too fat, too freckled, too pale, too dark, too young. Whatever you think are your shortcomings, you spend time and energy resisting. Rather than resisting, accept that you don't like whatever it is. Allow yourself to not like that particular thing. Just acknowledge that it is part of you. Then spend your energy on improving your Back Talk to the Voice that is doing the judging that's causing you so much pain. You may not be able to change the fact that you'll be wearing braces for two more years, but you can change the way you feel about wearing braces by being accepting and supportive of yourself.

Self-esteem is yours. You already have it. You may not know about it or use it, but it's yours. Self-esteem is inside you. Polly Perfect looked for things outside of herself to make her okay with herself. Peggy Pleezer was so busy trying to get everybody else to like her that she didn't have time to look and see what she liked about herself. Whenever you look to other people for your good feelings about yourself, it will never be enough. Your Voice will reject the positive and keep telling you to try harder because you're not good enough.

Get involved with your Inner Being. Believe it when it tells you what you value, what you believe in, what's good for you. Trust your feelings and maintain your integrity by being self-responsible, thinking for yourself and letting others know your thoughts and feelings through self-assertion.

Self-esteem: A Process, Not a Product

Self-esteem isn't a thing you get and then have forever. It's a process that evolves throughout your life. You'll have times when you feel confident, capable, and very competent. Other times you'll wonder where your self-esteem disappeared to. Harry Hardy was a good athlete and had lots of self-esteem when he was with the team. When Polly Perfect walked into his vicinity, his self-esteem became a 2 on a scale of 1 to 10. Felicia knew she was a good clarinet player and had high self-esteem around that. As an athlete her feelings of competence were very low. Harry and Felicia allowed their feelings in a few areas to affect the way they felt about themselves totally. It's that old 1 or 10 thinking. It's important to realize that 2 through 9 *do* count.

When you accept yourself as you are, you can look at the areas that need improvement and do something about them, but always give yourself credit for where you are. Look at your strengths and build on them. Peggy was a friendly, helpful person. On one hand, that caused her problems because she allowed others to take advantage of her. On the other hand, when she learns to set her limits, her friendliness and helpfulness will bring her satisfaction and enhance her self-esteem.

Missie Meek has always allowed others with unrealistic expectations to discount her hard work. By accepting herself as she is, she can give herself credit for her hard work and disagree with the unjust criticisms of others. When she bakes brownies and her mother wishes for chocolate chip cookies, Missie can feel good about her ability as a baker and enhance her self-esteem by saying, "These brownies are really good. Next time I'll do chocolate chip cookies." Becoming aware of her strengths and accepting her limitations will give Missie a realistic view of herself that will allow her to see herself in a more positive light.

Ms. Fauna may think that Missie only needs to try harder to get an A in zoology, but Missie knows she's done her best and getting an A is an unrealistic expectation for her. By accepting that, Missie has taken a step along the path to higher self-esteem. When Missie said she was going to start giving herself credit for her good points, she was saying that 2 through 9 count. She was ready to give up her all-or-nothing thinking. That's a giant step toward high self-esteem.

Because self-esteem is a process, it's not stable. It doesn't stay the same all the time. People with high self-esteem don't always feel enthusiastic, comfortable, and secure. Sometimes they feel sad, anxious, fearful, angry, insecure, and incompetent. They aren't always confident and sure about what they're doing. They accept those feelings and know that no matter what they're feeling, *they are okay people*. The source of approval for people with high self-esteem is from within rather than from without. They know and appreciate their values and beliefs and stand up for them. They know and trust their feelings and act on them assertively.

You have all you need to be the person you want to be. You can have as much self-esteem as you want to have. To have what you want for yourself in your life takes only the willingness on your part to look for it within yourself and to use what you find. No one can give you self-esteem. Since no one can give it to you, no one can take it away. Self-esteem is your choice—not your right, your choice.

Appendix

AFFIRMATIONS

Building and maintaining self-esteem requires care and nuturing. The way to do that is through affirmations. Affirmations are strong, positive statements about yourself that you believe or want to believe. Yes, want to believe. You may not believe them today, but if you repeat them enough, you will believe them. Affirmations are wonderful ways to replace the critical Voice. Read the list of affirmations every day and choose one to be yours for the day or the week. Add your own affirmations to the list. Listen for positive comments from others and put them on your list.

- I am a worthwhile person.
- I am important.
- I am beautiful inside and outside.
- I love myself unconditionally.
- I am capable of changing.
- I am a good person.
- I am loved because I deserve love.
- I can now practice being good to myself.
- I'm okay even if I'm not perfect.
- I accept myself—everything about me.
- I like who I am even though I don't always like what I do.
- I have many good qualities to offer.
- It's okay to make a mistake.
- I deserve to be happy.
- I don't need others to approve of me for me to approve of me.

- I like me.
- I respect myself.
- I treat myself and others with dignity and respect.
- I like the way I.......(Put in what fits for you.)
- I like my laugh.
- I like my sense of humor.
- I am a good brother/sister.
- I am a caring person.
- I am a very interesting person.
- I am okay even if I don't please others.
- It's okay to please myself.
- I am a responsible person.
- I am capable and confident.
- I am happy with myself.
- I am handling my problems effectively each day.
- I am free to be the best I can be.
- I feel good about myself.
- I'm okay today.
- I'm successful in school.
- I have everything I need to pass this test.
- I am prepared to do my best.
- I have satisfying relationships with others.
- I am a good friend.

Index